I0752824

THE LIFE OF SIR WILLIAM WALLACE,

THE

GOVERNOR GENERAL OF SCOTLAND,

AND HERO OF THE

SCOTTISH CHIEFS.

CONTAINING HIS PARENTAGE, ADVENTURES, HEROIC ACHIEVEMENTS, IMPRISONMENTS AND DEATH; DRAWN FROM AUTHENTIC MATERIALS OF SCOTTISH HISTORY.

BY PETER DONALDSON.

Chirurgeon, of the Store-Mount-Lock.

HARTFORD:
PUBLISHED BY S. ANDRUS & SON.

1851.

THE AUTHOR'S ADDRESS,

TO ALL TRUE HEARTED CALEDONIANS.

It appears no easy undertaking CALEDONIANS, to write the history and do justice to the character of the most illustrious General, consumate Statesman and courageous Warrior, that ever graced the pages of history, the invincible Hero of SCOTLAND, Sir WILLIAM WALLACE, the subject of the subsequent Memoir.

To give a just history of the life, adventures and heroic actions of that unparalleled Hero of Caledonia, who was equally qualified, by extraordinary natural endowments and martial acquirements, to excel in the administrations of the Cabinet and Tactics of the field, would require a character in letters equal to that of his hero in peace and in war, in the Court and in the field, no ordinary pen can do justice to the name of such a chieftain; no common intellect can value his merits; no ignoble soul can estimate the worth of such a conqueror; let the annals of Caledonia display his glories; let the pages of her histories speak forth his virtues; let her biographies depict the renowned character of their Hero: and let his magnanimous deeds be engraved on the memories of all her true-hearted patriots, as long as the sun shall endure.

In whatever light we view that illustrious warrior, emotions of love and glory will rise in our hearts, and will irresistibly lead us to behold him as an example worthy of imitation, and a subject of admiration either as a Christian or a Hero. This is the great reason I have for writing a history of the Chieftain, it being well known that example has a more powerful influence on the human mind than precept, as it predisposes to design, stimulates to action, and directs how to proceed with success, in the paths of virtue and glory. It awakens the dormant energies of the soul, and raises the spirits of men, to display the vigour of their minds, in the most exalted achievements.

The character of the illustrious Sir William Wallace is replete with exemplary virtues and heroic actions, which are both calculated to embolden the soul and impassion the heart of every true-blooded Scotsman. His patriotism, generotity, penetration, knowledge of human nature, address, courage, fortitude, perseverance, endurance and prudence, rank him among the greatest heroes of the world. Nay, such a degree of martial eminence distinguished his career, that it is impossible to select a warrior of ancient or modern times, who can equal him in greatness, or be compared to him in dignity and magnanimity.

The history of human nature, as it is exhibited in the Scottish character, amply demonstrates that no means have been more successful, no motive more powerful, to raise the native energy and to stimulate the native valour of Scotsmen, than to give a lively and accurate description of those wars in which their heroic fathers encountered dangers, endured hardships, braved death, nobly conquered or bravely died in defence of the rights and liberties of their native country. Is there a young Scotsman in existence, who glories in being a native of Scotland, that free and independent Caledonia, that can read the wonderful achievements of Sir William Wallace, and of those heroes who fought under his banner, without feeling a portion of that generous and magnanimous flame which fired his soul, directed his councils, and sharpened his claymore? Is there an aged Scotsman in existence, who glories in being a native of Caledonia, that can recount the glories of her chieftains and her warriors, without being fired with a love of his country? Can any Scotsman divest himself of this natural love and fight against his country? If there be any such among us, let them be deemed traitors to Caledonia. Awake! awake! to ancient sentiments of courage; display your native souls, ye true hearted sons of Caledonia? *Ruack, Ruack, Chebodi!*

You well know, Caledonians, that Sir William Wallace was the most noble and magnanimous of all the chieftains of Scotland; that he has been admired for his singular virtues and famous exploits, upwards of five hundred years, not only by those of his own nation, but kings, princes and people of distant countries of the earth courted his favour. And I am conscious, that his name will be recorded in the pages of our histories, and in the memories of his affectionate countrymen, till the consummation of the natural world. None of the heroes of antiquity, even in their poetical characters, shone with more illustrious virtues than did Sir William Wallace; none of the warrior's of Britain, ever merited the love, esteem, veneration and remembrance of his countrymen more than he has done in restoring their natural rights and liberties, in repairing the honour and glory of the nation, and in redressing their wrongs. All his superior wisdom, all his strength and valour of soul and body, were gratuitously employed in the services of his country. In his government he dispensed the laws of equity and justice, in his campaigns he procured their liberty and independence; in his administrations he preserved the people from the anarchy of sedition at home, and maintained their rights against the designs of foreign invasion.—He was the Friend of man, the Protector of their persons, the Preserver of their liberties and their laws, the Defender of their rights and Avenger of their wrongs. None in the thirteenth century was found a parallel to his character, none in the annals of human history or tradition had the welfare of their country nearer their hearts. Born the benefactor of his country he united all the qualities necessary for an illustrious career. Nature seems to have endued him with all the transcendant virtues of greatness, dignity, fortitude, integrity, benevolence, goodness and severity of soul, that endeared him to the hearts of all men; she endued him with such an amazing strength and hardiness of body too, that rendered him at once the glory of his companions in arms, and terror of his enemies in war. He was called by his country to the defence of her liberties; he nobly vindicated her rights, and triumphed gloriously over her enemies; he thrice delivered his country from the dominion of a foreign usurper; he thrice laid the pillars of her national independence on the foundations of unalterable equity and justice, with a wisdom in the cabinet equal to his glory in the field; and the love of his country shone conspicuously through all his administrations and achievements. He accepted the reins of government to save his country from a foreign invader; he wielded his Claymore to maintain her rights and liberties; he voluntarily resigned them to preserve her peace, and retired into the shades of a private life to heal her bleeding wounds. A spectacle so grand and sublime was contemplated by the people of different regions of the earth, with the profoundest admiration. The name of Wallace was revered by his friends and dreaded by his enemies; even kings of other nations courted his favour; the robbers of the ocean bowed to his invincible arm; the power of England was crushed by him, and his fame resounded from the uttermost boundaries of Europe and Isles of the ocean. His highest ambition was the happiness of his country, and the welfare of her sons. He was brave in his youth, invincible in battle, illustrious in all social virtues, unparalleled in magnanimity, and great in his death, bequeathing to posterity the inheritance of valour, which have been sufficient to raise a monument of esteem in the glowing hearts of his countrymen, in all succeeding ages. He lived the unrivalled ornament of his age, and departed in possession of the praises of an affectionate, mourning people.

The history of such a Hero will doubtless be hailed by all true-hearted Scots with joy. It will contain a circumstantial narrative of the most famous war, that ever occupied the sons and fields of Britain, carried on between the realms of England and Scotland for the space of forty years; the one unjustly invading, the other nobly defending the rights and liberties of devoted Caledonia. A war which produced amazing alterations both in the general government, and in the rising and falling of many families of distinction in the nation; the one betraying, the other maintaining her liberties and her laws. And to render the whole of the history of this renowned warrior complete and consistent, we shall here enumerate the causes, occasions, necessities, &c. of that war, in which our hero so nobly signalized himself as the just governor, the wise legislator, the benevolent protector of his country. When Alexander the III., king of Scotland, who terminated a succession of Princes that swayed the Scottish sceptre for the space of eight hundred years, was killed by a fall from his horse over the west craigs of Kinghorn, he left no issue of his body to succeed him on the throne, and his grand daughter Margaret of Norway, commonly called the Maid of Norway, became the nearest heiress to the crown. She being an infant at the time of the king's death, a Convention of the Estates of Parliament was held at Scone, and the immediate government of the kingdom was committed to the administration of Six Regents, William Frazer, Bishop of St. Andrews, Duncan Macduff, Earl of Fife, Alexander Cummin, Earl of Buchan, Robert Wiseheart, Bishop of Glasgow, John Cummin, Lord of Badenoch, and James Stewart, the Grand Steward of Scotland, who governed the realm for the space of seven years. During this period, Edward the I. King of England, knowing that his sister's grand daughter, child of the King of Norway, was the only surviving person of all the posterity of Alexander, as lawful heiress to the kingdom of Scotland, was ambitious, and sent Ambassadors to the Estates to desire Margaret of Norway in marriage for his eldest son, Edward, with a design to annex Scotland to the dominions of his crown.

Ambassadors from Edward of England, and Eric of Norway met at Bryham, near Shelson, on the 18th of July, 1290, with full powers to negotiate and settle the conditions of the marriage.—The Parliament agreed to the marriage, as being advantageous to the Kingdom; but they took good care in settling the conditions, that all provisions were made to secure the independence of the kingdom in case of death, and to guard against every danger that might arise from so near an alliance with so powerful and ambitious a monarch. In the matrimonial treaty it was stipulated that the Scots should enjoy their ancient laws, liberties and customs; that in case Edward and Margaret should be without any issue, the kingdom should return free, independent and absolute, to the next Scottish heir; that in case Edward should die before Margaret, without issue by her, the body of Margaret should be remitted to Scotland free and independent; that the military tenants of the crown, and other subjects, should not be obliged to do homage to him; to swear fealty; to elect or be elected to any office, or to do service in any place that had usually been performed in Scotland; that the kingdom of Scotland should have its Chancellor, Officers of State, Courts of Justice and all other public courts, as formerly; that a new great seal should be made and kept by the Chancellor, with the ordinary arms of Scotland, and the name of no one, but the Queen engraved upon it; that all papers and records belonging to the crown should be lodged within the Kingdom, that no duties, taxes or levies of men, should be raised in Scotland, but such as had been usual; that the King of England should pay the Pope one hundred thousand pounds, for the use of the Holy Wars; and that himself and his dominions should be excommunicated and laid under an interdict if he did not religiously observe all these Articles

These articles were agreed to and ratified by Edward. After reading those stipulations, which seemed to have been formed by the wisest heads and established on the surest foundations, who can say "that the Scots of those ages were an ignorant and barbarous people," as some have inferred? no better precautions could have been devised by the most enlightened statesman of posterior ages to secure the liberty and independence of the kingdom.

Treacherous Edward, Caledonians, did not hold his treaties sacred, and he violated his contract a short time after its ratification, by appointing one of his subjects to act in Scotland as Lieutenant for his son, requiring the Scots to deliver up all their Castles and strong holds into his hands, which clearly manifested his designs to wrest the terms of the treaty to answer the purposes of his ambition, regardless of the conditions of it, that were any wise unfavourable to his views. Edward to effect his ends in a more formal manner, applied to the Pope for a dispensation to sanction a marriage between his son and his good niece, the Maid of Norway, who was not yet marriageable. Having obtained his object and regained the friendship of the Scottish nobles, he joined with them in applying to the King of Norway, to ratify his treaty, by sending the young Queen home to her kingdom. The Norwegian King was unwilling to transmit his young child to the care of strangers, but the importunities and artifices of Edward and persuasions of the Scots, prevailed upon him to send his daughter. The fond hopes of the Scots and Edward were totally frustrated, in the death of the young Princess, on the Orkney Isles, where the Ambassadors were obliged to convey her on shore, on account of her sickness.

The Estates of Scotland soon perceived the coming confusion of a disputed succession, intestine discord, and an unavoidable war with the ambitious Monarch of England. The death of their young Queen bereaved them of the surest pledge of peace and liberty, and was attended with the most fatal consequences that ever followed the demise of the greatest personages.

In this disputed succession, two principal competitors out of thirteen, who seemed to have prospects of ascending the Throne, appeared first to enter their respective claims to the Kingdom. Deverguild the daughter of Margaret, the first daughter of David, Earl of Huntington; and Robert Bruce, the son of Isabel the second daughter of David, Earl of Huntington, respectively claimed the crown. Deverguild, because she was the nearest Heiress; the grand son of David, Bruce, because he was the nearest Heir, the grand son of David. Deverguild's pretensions were grounded on the custom of the country, whereby the nearest Heir or Heiress, descended from the same David, through an eldest daughter, and Bruce, insisted on the Sex, proving, that males, in equal degrees of propinquity of blood ought to be preferred before females; so he denied the justice of a grand daughter, inheriting the Kingdom, while a grandson, even of a second daughter was alive. Bruce also contended that he was a degree nearer in his claims to the throne, being a grandson, than John Baliol, who was only a great grandson; as for Deverguild, who stood in an equal degree, he was to be preferred to a female Heiress. The Scottish Parliament could not decide this controversy at home, because of the powers of each party, the whole land being divided in two equal factions, which although it should have been equitably determined by the Estates, would not have stood to the award, whence a civil war would have been the consequence. So they unanimously chose Edward, King of England, Umpire in Arbitration, in this important affair. The majority of the Arbitrators decided it in favour of John Baliol, although he was inferior in powers and popularity. Edward, knowing this circumstance went to Bruce, whom, being legally cast by their votes, he thought would accept of the crown under him. Bruce answered him in the following words., "I am not so eager of a crown as to accept of it, by abridging the liberty my ancestors have left me," and he was immediately dismissed.—Edward then offered the under-government of the realm to Baliol, who greedily accepted it under any condition he pleased to propose to him. So Baliol was crowned, and declared King of Scotland, at Scone, six years and nine months after the death of Alexander.

In a sno t time after the coronation of Baliol, Duncan Macduff, Earl of Fife, was murdered by the Abernethians, which was then a rich and powerful family, in Scotland, and who had previously accused Macduff's brother before the Assembly of Estates of depriving them of their lawful possessions: Baliol decided in favour of the Abernethians, and Macduff was thereby dispossessed of the lands in dispute. Macduff was doubly displeased at the partial King, because he was injured, and because the murderers of his brother were left unpunished. He immediately appealed to Edward and desired that Baliol might be made to answer before him, touching the matter and his decision; Baliol was not permitted in parliament to reply by proctor, but compelled to plead his own cause in a lower place of the house. He bore the affront silently for the present, but as soon as he departed, flames of anger and revenge burned in his breast. He occupied all his time for sometime afterwards, in conciliating the minds of his subjects, and in meditating revenge on Edward by a general revolt. Meantime a controversy arose between the French and the English, which terminated in a war. Embassies came from both nations; the French sent Ambassadors to renew the ancient league, the English sent them to demand aids from their Scottish Provincials, in the war. Both Embassies, were referred to the Council of the Estates, who, being prone to vindicate their independence, decided to renew the league with France, and to renounce all allegiance to England, and to retrieve the loss of their rights and liberties.

Edward immediately made a truce with the French in order to chastise the Scots, hoping to subdue them in a single campaign. Accordingly he sent his fleet, designed for France, against Scotland. The Scots attacked this fleet in the mouth of of the river Tweed, destroyed and took eighteen of their ships and put the rest to flight. Edward when he heard of this disaster, gave loose to his furious temper and breathed out revenge. Edward then carried a great army into Scotland, attacked Berwick, but could not take it. He then pretended to abandon the siege and caused a rumour to be spread by some Scots of Bruce's party, whom he himself had foste.ed, that he dispaired of carrying it, and that Baliol was coming with a large army to raise the siege. Upon which rumour all the chief men of the Scots garrison issued forth unsuspectingly to receive their King honourably, in a promiscuous multitude, horse and foot. At that fatal moment, Edward sent a company of horse among them and killed and rode them down, seized the nearest gate, and took the town.—Then he followed with his foot, and slaughtered all sorts of people. Seven thousand Scots were slain in that inauspicious day with all the flower of the nobility of Lothian and Fife. O ye credulous and unsuspecting Caledonians, why did you lay yourselves open to subtle Edward's stratagems! then Edward successively defeated the Scots, reduced all the garrisons, took Baliol, and sent him to the Tower of London. He then summoned all the surviving Nobles to attend him at Berwick, and compelled them to swear fealty to him, appointing John Warren, Commander in Chief, and Hugh Cressingham, Lord Chief Justice in his conquered Provinces of Scotland. During this state of subjection, when all the Castles and strong holds of the country were garrisoned by English soldiers, and the whole land groaned under a foreign usurpation for nine years, the noble soul of Sir William Wallace could not rest to see his country ravaged by sanguinary oppressors. Thus, when the nobility had neither power nor courage to undertake their own liberation, WILLIAM WALLACE, a man descended of an ancient and noble family, arose to restore her liberties and maintain her rights.

THE LIFE

ADVENTURES AND ACHIEVEMENTS,

OF THE CELEBRATED

SIR WILLIAM WALLACE,

GOVERNOR GENERAL OF SCOTLAND.

SIR WILLIAM WALLACE was descended of an ancient and noble family. He was the son of Sir Malcom Wallace, of Ellerslie, whose progenitors were the ancient knights and baronets of Craigie. His mother was daughter of Sir Ronald Crawford, High Sheriff of Ayre. He was born in 1288, during the reign of William, surnamed the Lion, and the usurpation of Donald, Lord of the isles. In his childhood, he lived with his parents at Ellerslie, and fled with them from place to place during Edward's nine years' usurpation and oppression, in domineering over them, when their country was reduced to a mere province under the martial laws of foreign invaders.

Sir William Wallace, even in his youth, before he arrived at the seventeenth year of his age, could not refrain from molesting the oppressors of his country. For, in 1302, when Edward cruelly oppressed the land, had destroyed all the ancient monuments and records, and shed much innocent blood, Malcom Wallace, the father of our hero, was forced to flee with his eldest son Malcom, into Lennox, among his relations, to avoid the fury of the English soldiers, and —— Crawford, his mother, retired to Kilspendie, in the Carse of Gowrie, upon the banks of the Tay, in Perthshire, and lived privately with her son William, in his uncle's house, during the time of war and bloodshed. Thence William Wallace was sent to Dundee, and was educated by John Blair, who afterwards became his chaplain, and lived to record his adventures. As he advanced towards his seventeenth year, he became a youth of uncommon sprightliness, gaiety, beauty, comeliness, and elegance, and endued with great agility and superior strength of body and mind. His peculiar dress distinguished him among the people and the oppressors of his country, who held the town of Dundee, and all other towns of the land by military garrisons, were the object of his hatred. He was clothed in garments of gemming green, had a Tartan bonnet on his head, a philabeig down to his knees, Tartan hose upon his legs up to the middle of the calves, and a plaid over his shoulders, according to the ancient custom of the Scottish nation. Indeed he was a noble and comely youth, both in dignity of soul and majesty of stature, in vigour of intellect, and singular strength of body. When he arrived at the 30th year of his age he was full nine quarters high in stature, three quarters broad between the shoulders; had big, well-shaped, brawny limbs; a strong, sonorious voice; burning brown hair; light eyebrows, quick, piercing, bright eyes; long, round and well-proportioned visage; a neat square nose; round ruddy lips; a high breast; a thick strong neck; large long arms, with swinging hands; a fine sanguine colour in countenance; a beautiful face; with becoming gravity of speech ; mildness in peace and fierceness in war, that distinguished him from the rest of mankind.

On Wallace's virtues, and his person rare,
None in his age could e'er with him compare.

His strength was equal to two of that of Robert Bruce, and the strength of Bruce was equal to that of any other two highland Scots. His sword was a strong, long, massy, broad claymore, of the best tempered steel, about five feet in length, made to be wielded with both hands occasionally, well calculated to sweep the field of battle, and make dreadful chasms in the ranks of his enemies. He always wore a steel cap and helmet on his head ; an armour of the closest and best workmanship ; two gloves of steel ; a close habergeon : an orby shield of impenetrable material ; a dagger hanging at his belt ; and all covered with a mantle, plaid cloak, or priest's gown in disguise, when he lurked in the hills, and spied places and parties of his enemies. He had no harness for his face, choosing rather to leave it bare for the shield's and claymore's defence.

Young Wallace, even in his youth, before he was able to wield his broad claymore or glittering spear, grieved at the injuries done to his country by their cruel oppressors. His soul boiled with inward rage at their barbarities, and he was fired with the passion of avenging the blood of his countrymen, and the pol lution of his countrywomen, whom the English had killed or ravaged in all parts of the land. " Alas, said Wallace, shall my country suffer such tyranny, and shall the Southerons daily increase to devour the residue of our fields, possess our habi 'ions, cities, towns, villages, deflour our maidens and kill our sons? Oh that I had ten thousand at my command, I, even I in my youth, would crack their curpons," and began to contend with individual Saxons, and often deprived them of their lives in open combat, as the subsequent history will show.

One day, it happened before he left Dundee, just at the commencement of his martial career, that an insolent young Englishman, the son of Selbie, the Constable of the town, insulted him and attempted to wrest his knife from him, uttering the following insult, "Scot what the de'il clad you in a suit so gay, a horse's mantle is the apparel of your kind, and a Scot's whittle at your belt rough roulin shoes, or any common trash, serve such whore's sons, to plash through the dubs ; give me that knife, hanging under thy girdle," and immediately endeavoured to snatch it from him by force ; but Wallace would not be deprived or robbed of his knife, and replied, "Nay, pardon me, Sir, I know better things, forbear, I entreat thee, it both defends me and cuts my meat." Young Selbie, however, would not desist, and Wallace would not be insulted and robbed of his knife, neither could he endure such an affront or insult with impunity. He seized young Selbie by the collar and instantly dispatched him on the spot, in the midst of his companions. The guard pursued him in great fury to avenge the death of the young squire at the expense of the blood of Wallace, who being amazingly strong and swift of foot, escaped out of their hands, sparing none who attempted to stop his flight.

The Saxons keenly pursued him, and being exhausted with running he rushed into an Inn, which he knew to be a harbour for the oppressed Scots, crying, "Help, help, save my life from cruel Southeron law," the good woman of the house, who perceived his dangerous predicament, quick as lightning dressed him in a russet gown, covered his head with an old soiled curch, put a white worn cap on his head over all, and set him down to spin, just as the furious soldiers entered the house in search of him; she gave him the rock and the distaff, and he began to spin and sing, and appeared totally indifferent at the sudden appearance of the Saxon guards in search of Wallace. There he hummed his song and spun, until they departed to some other place in pursuit of him; then he revived—he laughed and rejoiced at his own escape, and in their disappointment.

The guards then ran up and down like furious madmen, crying "Burn the Scots, burn the Scots, leave none of them alive in town;" but the good woman kept young Wallace until night, secured him from the hand of the Southerons; and in the morning long before day conveyed him secretly through a back path which led privately along the rivulet, which ran through the town, and he quickly escaped to his uncles retreat in the Carse of Gowrie.

Meantime his mother having heard of the great peril of her son, her beloved young William, despaired of his life among the cruel Southerons, and proceeded in all haste and anxiety to see what became of him. To her great surprise and joy she met him hasting to Kilspindie. The benevolent old parent could not refrain from tears, when he began to tell her of dispatching young Selbie, the pursuit of his enemies, and his providential escape from their sanguinary hands; she exclaimed in expressions of dread, gladness and sorrow, "Oh bless me, my son, can I believe mine eyes? is it possible that you havé passed the danger? sure Providence is more than kind in the last extremity of fortune." And as he informed her of his dangerous situation she wept and often said in sighs and tears, "Alas! my son, ere you leave off your pranks thine enemies will fang thee." "Mither," answered young Wallace, "I would rather see them hanged upon a tree, methinks we should withstand these Southeron oppressors, that possess our land." His aged uncle soon received the doleful news of Selbie's death and of Wallace's peril; was filled with grief, and dreaded the consequence of such a rash act to the adventurous youth. Meantime the English held a court of Justice at Dundee and prepared to avenge the death of their squire Selbie on the heads of the Scots, and Wallace could sojourn no longer at Kilspindie with his uncle, in the Carse of Gowrie. His mother clothed herself in the garments of a pilgrim, and disguised her son, and departed in great haste to their relations in Dunipace, in Sterlingshire, where a great Parson of an opulent estate, a devout man, named Richard Wallace, his paternal Uncle, who entertained them with every kind of hospitality and con versation, about the great tribulations of the land, intreating them to remain with him, till God should send better days. But brave Wallace replied in the ardour of his soul, "I hasten to the west, our kind kindred are massacred there; were I at home I would be avenged on the English for the blood of my relations." The grave old Parson sighed in goodness, saying, "I doubt that it will be long e'er that time come; "come weal, come woe," answered Wallace,

"I will pursue my purpose." The old man inculcated the national maxim on his mind, i. e. "that liberty was the best of human blessings, and that without it life was not worth enjoying," which cherished the best of his genuis, and matured those dispositions which were to bless his country, and gain him the laurels of immortal fame; and he bade his uncle "Adieu." Wallace and his mother winged their flight to Ellerslie, and in the morning sent for Sir Ronald Crawford, her brother, who informed them, with sorrow of heart and tears, that her husband, and her eldest son, William's father and brother, were slain by the cruel English soldiers. He told them of the valour of Malcom Wallace; how he hewed the English down after his hough sinews were cut, and Malcom, the younger, who fell in the field of Lochmaben, in defence of their country. The soul of young William was fired on that relation with love and glory, and desire of vengeance; and he secretly designed to retaliate on the heads of the English at some future period, when time and opportunity should serve his ends.

Mrs. Wallace, his mother, persuaded Sir Ronald Crawford, her brother, to petition Lord Percy, then Lieutenant General of Scotland, for permission to live quietly at Ellerslie, for she was bowed down with sorrow and cares in a good old age. Sir Ronald obtained a protection for his sister, but William Wallace disdained to remain under their protection, and proceeded to Richardstown, and lived some time with his uncle Sir Richard Wallace, who had been a warrior of great valour, renown, wisdom and opulence. Wallace arrived at his uncles house in February, and in April went out for diversion and amusement, to angle in the water of Irvine, not dreading the attack of his enemies. But, having fished successfully for some hours, accompanied with a boy to carry the bag, Lord Percy and his suite came riding along, and excited some degree of uneasiness in the mind of Wallace, because he had forgot to bring his sword with him. Five of Percy's guards in green uniform, mounted on their troopers, advanced to Wallace, and in blustering language accosted him with tyrannical expressions, "Zounds Scot, we shall have thy fish." Wallace in graceful modesty replied, "I will share the half with you most cheerfully." But one of them answered, "that would be too little," and alighted and snatched them all from the boy. Then Wallace said "I am sure in modesty you will leave us some, if ye are gentlemen; let an aged Knight that lives in yonder house, have some, pray be so generous." The English robber answered, "you clown, the river has enough in store, we serve a lord, who shall dine upon these ere long." Wallace replied in burning vengeance, "Thou art in the wrong, whom hast thou nere, faith thou deservest a blow;" the Southeron then began to abuse Wallace, saying "poor prattling Scot, how darest thou talk so contemptuously," and rushed on Wallace with his drawn sword, but Wallace being dexterous and strong parried it off with his pole-staff and laid him on the ground, snatched up his sword and with one back stroke clave his neck in two. The other four pillagers, when they saw their companions slain in their presence, alighted from their horses, rushed upon Wallace with all their united force, and completely surrounded him; but

Wallace nobly stood his ground, against the four in arms, and fiercely struck at one upon the head, and his glancing Claymore cut through his collar-bone; he struck another on the arm and laid both hand and sword on the ground together; another he slew with a back sweep of his sword, and the other two fled for their lives. The silly cowards informed Lord Percy, that three of their comrades were slain, and he saw their own two bloody heads, and asked them how many enemies they had encountered. They answered "ONE." "A devil surely," replied Percy, "since one has killed three and put two to flight, cowardly coxcombs pack ye out of my sight. It seems the Scot has fought most manfully for me this day, in faith he shall not be sought; was ever such a defeat heard of before in any land, ye whore's son's birds, let a Scots pole staff command five English swords."

Meantime Wallace mounted one of the Southeron horses, and carried the other two along with him to Richardtown, to his uncle. The good old knight was surprised at the news of Wallace's encounter and victory, and almost fainted in the presence of his intrepid nephew; counselled him to keep it secret, con cluding that "for such fishing sports you may pay dearly, if it should be known." "Uncle," said the undaunted Wallace, "I will push my fortune now where I can expect success, since I can no longer evade the eye of mine enemies, I will try the English geldings how they ride." The good old man consented, and gave him a purse of gold. Wallace kneeled down and humbly took his leave, and the aged knight holding him by the hand, said in love and affection, "when that is done send for more, I pray my dear nephew, and God speed."

Firm to his resolution he spared neither great nor small of the English, who fell in his way. For those heroic actions he was out-lawed by them and compelled during the inclement winter of 1207, to live in the fields, the woods, the mountains and the dens of the earth, where he wandered exposed to all the hardships and privations that human nature could possibly sustain. The ardent love of freedom, and his implacable hatred of the English oppressors of his country, harrowed up all the passions of his soul, and as an eagle hunting for his prey, he panted for revenge upon their heads. He lost no opportunity to attack them by surprise, while he lurked in the woods and mountains.

WALLACE KILLS THE BULLY WITH ONE STROKE OF HIS OWN STAFF, IN AYRE.

After the angling exploit, Wallace withdrew a little while to Ochter-house and Longland-wood, to avoid the fury of his enemies. When the rumour of his fishing sport was supposed to have vanished, he repaired to the town of Ayre, in disguise, to reconnoiter his enemy's security and exposures. He alighted from his horse in Longlandwood, and gravely walked to the cross in the town of Ayre, where Lord Percy commanded the garrison of Englishmen; appeared nothing daunted; walking briskly round, and viewed all the barbarous crew, wallowing in luxuries and the spoils of his country. Wallace could scarce restrain his passion and youthful ardour against the cruel invaders and oppressors of his beloved country. But to divert his attention from manifesting his hatred to the enemy, Wallace went to see a huge English clown, who boasted greatly of his matchless strength, and who challenged the Scots at the bearing of burdens, and blows on his body. As Wallace approached him to see the sport, "I will bear a greater burden," said the prince of sots, "than any three good sturdy Scots, or I will permit and bear a blow with a staff like a stage dancer's pole for one single groat from the hand of the strongest Scot." He could not refrain from laughing at the temerity of the fool, and said to the Champion of the Southerons, "I am ready and willing for one Scot's blow, to give an English shilling." The wretch immediately accepted of the money and soon reaped the fruits of his folly; for Wallace being actually endowed with the strength of four ordinary Scots, gave him such a blow on the back that clave his rig bone, and he instantly sunk in death. A solemn silence prevailed like a calm before a storm, for a few minutes, till the guards of the town were informed of the death of their Champion. The Southerons armed with swords and spears immediately surrounded him; but still he appeared undismayed in this perilous situation, he cocked his steel bonnet and began to defend himself by the same staff with which he killed the churl. At the first blow he dashed out the brains of one, struck another's bayonet and killed him. The staff was split and riven by its collision with the steel of his enemy; but happily he had a sword concealed within the skirt of his garment, which he immediately drew with awful grace and majesty and swung the trusty steel to clear his way towards his steed. In cutting through the host of numerous foes he was sorely pressed in the rear by two strenuous warriors. His anger was kindled, and like a lion in his strength he turned his eyes and swung his weighty Claymore, slew the foremost, and clave the second down through the body. Five Southerons were laid dead upon the ground, all killed by one bold Scot, in the midst of hundreds of his enemies. In the mean time Wallace having cleared and forced his way, mounted his trusty steed and scampered off to Longlandwood, pursued by companies of horse and foot. In the thicket of the wood he eluded the search and sight of his enemies, and was supplied with provisions and all necessaries from Ochter-house, during his concealment in Longlandwood. Wallace having become impatient in his lurking place, and being desirous of reviewing the garrison of the enemy, returned in disguise to Ayre. But ah! it proved a fatal day, I wish to Jove that he had stayed away.

WALLACE KILLS LORD PIERCY'S STEWARD AND IS TAKEN PRISONER.

As Sir Ronald Crawford's servant was buying fish for his master in the market of Ayre, Lord Percy's steward came and assaulted him in terms of the greatest disdain. "Scot," said the steward, "for whom buyest thou these fish thou carriest." The servant answered, "Sir, for the Sheriff of Ayre." "By heaven's king," the steward rudely swore, "my lord shall have them, and thou mayest purchase more." Wallace overhearing the conversation, was incensed with the insulting rudeness and insolence of this pirating steward over the humble Scots servant, and could no longer restrain his indignation; "why such rudeness, tell the reason why?" demanded Wallace, and the haughty steward's blood began to boil with rage and he replied, "go hence thou saucy Scot, with speed, I mock thee and thy sheriff," and smote Wallace with his hunting-staff; but alas! for the poor devoted steward, better for him that he had kissed the foot of the Scot, and asked his pardon, for Wallace drew his mighty claymore and despatched him in the twinkling of an eye. In an instant a crowd assembled and eighty of the guards, well armed, surrounded Wallace, who stared at them and never uttered a word; but boldly drew his daring claymore and dashed through the ranks of his compassing enemies, transfixed the foremost through the body, cut the leg of the second at the knee and severed the head from the body of the third in the three resistless sweeps of his tremendous claymore. Thus he raged like a lion among his enemies, cutting his way towards the gate; but alas! the enemy were strongly posted at the gate with swords and spears to prevent his escape. Then in desperation he hewed them down like silly sheep, and even when they environed him with countless numbers he stalked through them like a living statue of iron, and placed himself at a wall near the sea, where none dare approach him, until the whole garrison issued forth to overpower and capture a single Scots warrior. They mounted on a dyke and broke down the wall, which defended Wallace's back, and left him no other shift but to fight or die. His soul was fired with double rage and he suddenly hewed down great numbers of his surrounding enemies, and fiercely passed through them.

But ah ! unlucky hour and fatal day ; his broad claymore broke off at the hilt, and the small dagger that was in his possession was not sufficient to cope with English spears and lengthy swords. He slew three of them with his dagger before they could overpower him with their numbers, swords, bayonets, and spears. The command was given not to slay him, but to take him alive, that they might starve him in a loathsome dungeon until they should bring him to a cruel and ignominious death, which, says the historian, resembled the prison of Hell. All Scots patriots and his personal friends wept for the fall of their mighty chieftain ; all mourned the fate of their beloved Wallace; in vain did piteous tears flow from the eyes of a mourning people ; none was able to release the hopes and glory of the nation ; and the weeping and the lamentation of the wives and children, as well as the patriots of Scotland, were sufficient to rend a heart of stone. Alas ! said they, can life endure to see our Wallace imprisoned and massacreed by the cruel enemies of our country ? the flower of youth in sweet and tender age, pine in a loathsome dungeon ? can we survive the death of our deliverer and protector ? and who in Scotland is left to defend her rights, liberties and her laws."

THE IMPRISONMENT AND ESCAPE OF WALLACE AT AYRE, IN AN EXTRAORDINARY MANNER.

During Wallace's imprisonment, the Southerons fed him on herrings and water, and offals of their shambles in the manner they would feed their dogs and swine, until death was pictured in his beauteous clay; all his vital spirits done and his soul sunk within him. Whereupon in expectation of immediate death he solemnly addresses the God of Mercy and Justice, imploring his pardon and favour on the footing of the propitiation of Jesus Christ, the Saviour of the world, in the following strain "O my God, may it please thee to receive my soul into the arms of thy sovereign mercy, or quickly loose me from the bands of this death, as seemeth good unto thy glorious Majesty. Give not up this oppressed nation into the hands of their cruel enemies, deliver them by thy mighty hand and rescue them by thine arm from the snares of their malicious foes," &c. Having uttered this prayer he turned his lamentation on the great cause of his defeat, saying "O brittle sword, thy metal was not true, the breaking of thy blade threw me into this dungeon and subjected thousands of gallant Scots; I trusted to thee, alas! thou hast failed me; I thought to have avenged the blood of my gallant father and noble uncle, and beloved brother upon the Southerons, who massacreed them at Lochmaben; but alas! for my dear country, which is doomed by this mischance to oppression and slavery." A cruel flux of the belly came on and consumed the poor remains of strength in the person of Wallace, and reduced him to the brink of the grave. When they saw that Wallace would soon die, they commanded the executioner to bring him to the sentence of the law The jailor having come and found Wallace, already dead, returned in great haste and reported his death. They all concluded to throw him over the castle wall as they do with the bodies of their dead dogs. But mysterious Providence, ever mindful of her favourites, directed his fall in a soft place without the wall, so that his bones were not broken. There Wallace lay motionless and apparently lifeless, until the news of his death and disgraceful funeral had reached the ears of his old nurse who lived in Ayre, and came running to ask permission to bear away the corpse of Wallace to burial. And having obtained permission, she carried his body home to her own house, bathed it in warm water, and to her great surprise and joy she felt his heart began to beat or flutter, and saw his eyes open in her presence. She immediately laid him on a soft bed and caused her daughter to suckle him with her own milk, until he recovered strength, and was able to walk out to meet his enemies.

All this time she nourished him with good nutriment and good solace, weeping in the presence of his enemies, and rejoicing in the presence of his friends, to quiet the one and console the other.—Thomas the rhymer, at that time prophecied in ancient Scottish rhyme, and was held in great estimation. He came to the parish priest to talk of the troubles and calamities of their country, and just when Thomas was there, the priest's servant returned from the market of Ayre, and told, that he had seen good young Wallace cast for dead over the castle wall.—The priest replied with a heavy heart, "I hope to see the Southerons smart for that cruel deed on the life and body of noble Wallace." Thomas observed the news were bad, and added, " Wallace is not dead," and paused in pensive thought, " The God, who hath made the world, and brings all things to pass for his own glory, if Wallace be dead, dooms Thomas to live no more." The priest sent his servant to the woman's house to know for certainty of the life or death of Wallace. The servant prayed to be introduced into the chamber where Wallace lay, and the woman led him up stairs and shewed him Wallace alive. The servant, as soon as he saw the majesty of his person, returned in great haste, and told his master and Thomas the glorious news of Wallace's life, health and safety. Then Thomas began again to prophecy of the greatness and glory of Wallace, that he would sweep the Southerons from the land, that thousands would fall at his right hand, that he should thrice deliver Scotland, and be the scourge of Southerons : then cheer up, ye Scots, cast off your care, and believe what he should now declare.

BATTLE OF LOUDOUN-HILL,

Fought by Wallace to revenge the slaughter of his Father and Brother.

As soon as Wallace recovered from his sickness produced by his imprisonment, he sent his nurse and her daughter who suckled him, with the rest of the family to Ellerslie, and prepared himself for war.—In all his preparations he could not find a sword to please him, except an old rusty blade which stood in the corner of the house, none seemed to be worth the carrying. He drew it out of the scabbard and found that it would bite keenly, and was wonderfully pleased with it, saying, "Faith thou shalt go with me, till I can procure a better," and immediately proceeded to Richardtown to procure a horse and armour, that he might be able to encounter the English Knights, who were all clothed in steel and accoutred with shining arms.

As he ventured to travel to Richardtown, three Southerons riding into Ayre, met him, Longcastle and two yeomen, who attempted to bring him back to Ayre; but Wallace drew back and would not be compelled to return. They turned furiously upon him, and despitefully accosted him, saying, "Thou Scot, stay, for surely thou art a spy or some thief, that darest not show your face." Wallace answered, "Sir, for God's sake let me alone, I am sick:" Longcastle replied in compulsatory language, "By George, thy countenance prognoisticates something odd! to Ayre, thou shalt go with me," pulling out his glittering sword to compel him to return. Wallace, who knew not fear, also drew his rusty blade, and with a single, but a dreadful blow, cut off Longcastle's head; the yeomen then rushed on him with the utmost fury; but Wallace stood like a post of iron and smote the foremost on the head and clove it down to the neck; whereupon the other fled to tell the doleful news. But Wallace, knowing that his escape would reveal his proceedings, pursued him, and gave him such a blow on the ribs, that all his lungs and entrails hung out of his body. He then seized their horses and their armour, their swords and their purses, the lawful spoil of a well fought field, mounted one of their horses, and rode on to Richardtown.

There Sir Richard Crawford rejoiced to see his nephew, and Sir Ronald soon joined the joyful company with his cheeks bedewed with tears. Sir Ronald held Wallace by the hand and kissed him in the joyful extacy of his soul, " Welcome, welcome, my dear nephew," said he, " welcome home to me ! thanks be to God who has brought thee out of prison and has rescued thee from the cruel hands of thy mortal enemies." All his kinsfolks, his mother and friends, assembled with joyful hearts to see beloved Wallace, who was dead and is alive again. Robert Boyd and a great number of his dearest friends and companions from all parts convened to rejoice with them on the re-appearance of their promising Chieftain.

As soon as Wallace obtained a select band of faithful companions in war, he proceeded in the month of July, to Machlein Muir, in order to wait an opportunity to avenge the death of his father, brother, uncle, &c. The three sons of Sir Richard, Adam, Richard, Simeon, all brave and bold ; Robert Boyd, Cleland, and Edward Little accompanied Wallace as chiefs in this expedition. At Machline Muir they were informed that Fenwick was on his route to Ayre, conveying waggons loaded with provisions and rich spoils from Carlisle. The soul of Wallace was elevated to hear of this noble purvey, and he inwardly strained to catch the prize. To Loudoun, then, these seven noble warriors, with forty-three at their command, all clothed in bright armour and accoutered with glitter ing claymores, briskly rode, and lodged all night in Loudoun's braes, where they were informed by a true-hearted Scot near Loudoun, that the provision waggons of Fenwick were in Annadale, and that the advanced guard had passed on to Ayre. Wallace knowing the course of their route, immediately ordered his worthy Scots to move at break of day to an advantageous ground, to lie in ambush for the approach of Fenwick, sending out two of their number to reconnoitre the plains. The Scots soon returned, and reported the coming of their enemies. All their horses were turned loose, with a determination to conquer or die ; and they fell on their knees to implore the God of power to protect them and the broken rights of Scotland. Prayers being ended, Wallace addressed his men to the following effect, " Here was my dear father and brother slain ! I shall be avenged on the head of the traitor that committed the felon deed," and commanded them to advance upon the hill. Fenwick saw them, and cried, " Yonder is Wallace ! I know him well : he lately broke our prison, and shall soon be captured again ; I shall not permit him to speak—his head will please our king better than gold, lands, or earthly things," and ordered his servant to stop his carriage until he should clear the way of his enemies. Nine score he led in bright burnished harness, and fifty on horseback.—The Scots on foot, armed with good claymores, and caps of steel, met them on the hill ; and oh ! to see the fury of the tremendous combat ! steel clashing against steel—legs and arms, brains and entrails covering all the plain, and the dying enemies lying weltering in their gore. Fenwick, never doubting victory, attempted to ride down the band of Scots by a furious onset; but Wallace, first in fight, met them fell and keen, with his immovable company of youths, and transfixed the foremost of the enemy: then all swords were drawn on either side, and were wielded in dire array. The Englishmen surrounded the Scots on every side thinking to bear them down by their horses and their numbers; but the close little band of Scots stood impenetrable, and repulsed all the attacks of their enemies. When Fenwick then saw their unexpected repulse, and the fields died with the blood of his men, he advanced on a prancing steed, clothed in bright armour; wielding the dreadful spear, with dismal gloom and dashed into the thickest of the fight in fury. Wallace saw the murderer of his parent and brother, and became as outrageous as a hungry lion; he flew at him, and with a deadly blow sheared away his thigh. 'Ere he was dead the enemy bore so close and keen, that poor Robert Boyd was almost overpowered by the number of his foes; but Wallace saw the unequal struggle of his noble companion, turned in again and rescued him from danger, and chased them through the plain. There Adam Wallace and Beaumont cut a Southeron Squire of great renown through the middle, and before night there was not a Southeron to dispute the field of battle. Three Scots Warriors fell in battle on that awful day; one hundred Southerons lay dead around them and four score escaped by flight, leaving all their convoy a prey to the victorious Scots.

The convoy consisted of gold, harness, horses, victuals, wines, even ten score of harnessed horses, besides provender and other things.

The vanquished Southerons fled to Ayre, and told Lord Piercy of their dismal disaster; how Wallace hanged their men on the trees of Clyde's wood, what numbers were slain in battle, &c. which greatly raised the fears and dread of Piercy respecting the power and vengeance of Wallace, and induced him to make overtures of peace.

THE ENGLISH MAKE PEACE WITH WALLACE.

In order to have time to receive reinforcements, and effect his destruction, devised a plot to ensnare him during the peace.

Wallace having won a glorious victory over the enemies of his country, and avenged the blood of his kindred on the heads of their murderers, retired to the green wood of Clyde with his adventurous companions.

Piercy in the mean time, proceeds to Glasgow, and summoned a council of the Lords temporal to devise how they might ensnare Wallace by some deep stratagem; for not one of their ten thousand men would go out against the mighty chieftain of Scotland, on account of the general rumour and dread of his name and power. In this secret council of war, Sir Aymer Vallance, the false and murderous knight of Bothwell, proposed a bloody plot to entrap and massacre him, by employing his nearest relations to influence him to a truce, by imposing upon his goodness and gentleness, especially through the persuasion of Sir Ronald Crawford, his beloved uncle. They threatened to confiscate all his lands, and to carry him to the prison of London; which the good old knight repelled by urging the impossibility of the undertaking, on the consideration of their having destroyed the kindred of Wallace. And when they could not prevail by menaces on Sir Ronald Crawford to use his influence to bring Wallace to conclude a peace, they promised him the Sheriffdom of Ayr. Alas! fair promises of honour and advancement overcame the good old knight, and he undertook the mediation on the conditions proposed by Piercy.

Sir Ronald then proceeded to the woods of Clyde, and drew near Wallace as he dined and feasted on the dainties and luxuries of their spoils, sat down and shared their merriment. After dinner, Sir Ronald declared his errand, " Nephew, said he, take my ad vice and counsel, make a truce for a season with the Southerons, otherwise all thy kindred will be slain." Wallace replied, " I shall make no peace with the oppressors of my country and the murderers of her sons." But Robert Boyd, to save the worthy knight, moved for peace; Cleland and Adam Wallace seconded the motion, and Wallace reluctantly agreed to proclaim peace, in hopes of future opportunities of liberating his country from the cruel yoke of their enemies, and they parted sadly on the plain. This happened in the month of August, 1296, in the 20th year of the age of Wallace.

WALLACE KILLS THE BUCKLER PLAYER IN THE TOWN OF AYRE

Wallace could not rest contented at Crosbie with Sir Ronald Crawford, to see his country's wrongs unredressed. He longed to see the town of Ayre, and he selected fifteen men, and proceeded to it in disguise. At the gate they met an English Fencer, boasting of the weapon, with a buckler in his hand. Wallace stood to see the play, and while he remained there, the Fencer challenged him to fight; "Scot, said he, darest thou try a stroke?" "Yes," said Wallace, "smite on, thy motion I defy," and immediately swung his dreadful claymore at his head, and clove it down to his shoulders, and returned to his men without the least concern. The women hallooed, "our Fencer is dead! our Fencer is slain!" and in a few moments fierce men in arms encompassed them; eight score now attacked sixteen, but Wallace ever fearless and foremost, with one dreadful blow, shattered the brains of the one opposed to him through his helmet, swung his awful claymore through the body of another, and cleared a space to wield resistless weapons; so did all his brave men, and great was the slaughter made among their assailants, ere reinforcements could be sent from the castle.—Wallace saw their design to surprise him, ordered his men to cut through their enemy's ranks, and hewing heads and brains asunder, wheeled round his men, appeared in the rear, and cleared a way for escape from their merciless enemies. The great hero and his men mounted their horses and galloped off to Longlandwood, leaving 29 Southerons dead in the gates of the city. Three kinsmen of lord Piercy, who were clothed in bright armour, paid the great debt of nature on that fatal day. Piercy then immediately accused Sir Ronald Crawford of a breach of faith, in a letter, because Wallace, he said, had not kept the peace. Wallace stayed seventeen days at Crosbie with his uncle, and promised to keep the peace, until the truce was ended. Sir Ronald showed him the letter of Piercy, and intreated him to remain quietly with him in his house; but the soul of Wallace was fired with passion against the cruel tyranny of the Southerons, who possessed his country.

WALLACE WINS THE PEEL OR FORT OF GARGUNNOCK.

In September, the English Peers convened in Council at Glasgow, and good Sir Ronald Crawford Sheriff of Ayre, behooved to be among them. So he proceeded on his journey to Glasgow, accompanied by William Wallace his nephew, and three servants.—On their way, they met a convoy of three horsemen and two footmen, with Piercy's baggage, who robbed Sir Ronald's servants upon the plain of all their master's property; and Sir Ronald himself never opposed them for the sake of peace; but Wallace saw the foul deed, and could not forgive the injury. He withdrew from the company of Sir Ronald, burning with anger, and vowing vengeance within his own breast, to waylay the rapacious monsters, who had perpetrated the robbery. He overtook them near Cathcart, and attacked them, brandishing his great claymore. The first sweep he made with his sword, severed the head from the shoulders of the foreman; three more of his companions quickly shared the fate of death by his claymore, and the fifth fled in great consternation. Wallace seized all their baggage and goods, and escaped into Lenox, leaving his friends to lament his absence, where he was courteously receiv ed by Malcom, the great Earl of Lenox. But Wallace could not remain idle while his native and groaned under a foreign yoke; grieved for their miserable condition, and resolved to raise an army to combat the enemies of his beloved country in the field. Stephen of Ireland, an exile of his country, entered into a league with Wallace; so did Faudon, a man of dreadful size and aspect, of iniquitous eyes, never smiled, and was fearful to the sight, who delighted in blood and battery. With these and other sixty brave Scots warriors, he marched northward, and surprised the garrison on Gargunnock hill, in the dead of the night; killed the watchmen, the captain and all the men in arms, only saving the women and children, and divided all the gold and provisions among his brave companions, who regaled themselves for four days in great profusion, on the spoils of their enemy; but Wallace fought for Scotland, and for glory. In the fifth day after the reduction of this fortified store house, they pursued their march across the Teth and Ern, in order to discover the motions, strength, or weakness of their enemies, and lodged in Methvin forest, where they could subsist upon hunting, and would not be compelled to fast and fight, as they had done in many places of resort.

WALLACE ENTERS ST. JOHNSTOUN, SLAYS THE CAPTAIN, AND WINS THE CASTLE OF KINCLEVEN.

He obtained admittance into the town, in disguise, with seven men, in the following manner. Having arrived at the gate, and demanded permission to enter, he was refused admittance, until the Provost was sent for to examine the strangers. When he saw Wallace, a tall strong man, he fixed his eyes upon him, suspected his huge appearance, and enquired whether they were all Scotsmen. Wallace readily answered, "we are not only all Scotsmen, but, as it is time of peace, there is no cause to refuse us admission." "This I grant," said the Provost, "and men of peace should always be well treated; but pray, tell me your name, and from what part of the country you are come?" Wallace answered, "my name is William Malcom, we come from Ettrick Forest, in the Scuth, to seek better employment in the North, and to see the country." The Provost then apologised for his suspicious inquiries, adding that he meant no harm by his questioning of them, excusing himself by saying, "that so many reports had been circulated about one William Wallace, born in the West, who was slaying or destroying the English wherever he could find them, therefore, as he was a tall, strong man, it was necessary to know those whom they admitted into the town." Wallace professed to know nothing about William Wallace, and desired the Provost not to mention such a hated name; and he was not only admitted into town, but had an inn provided for him and his men, until they should find employment, and were provided with every thing the place afforded. He often invited Englishmen to drink with him, on purpose to discover their number and strength of the place; his great business being to spy out their positions, in order to surprise them, or burn the town.

Wallace could not venture to set it in flames, on account of the difficulty of escape; but then he discovered, that Sir James Butler, an aged knight, who kept the castle of Kincleven, resided in town, with Sir John, his son, an under captain to Sir Gerard Heron, then commander of the garrison; and was about to return to that strong hold, with a guard of 90 well armed horsemen, chosen men of valour. Wallace on hearing this report of Sir James's return to Kincleven castle, hastened off to Mithvinwood, blew his martial horn and all his intrepid warriors quickly assembled round him, all blooming in good health, and ready for action, at the command of their leader.

He then marched his well armed little band from the woods in a valley along the banks of the sweet winding Tay, and, at a short distance from Kincleven lay in ambush among the bushes, and sent spies in different directions, to reconnoiter their approach.—Some of them soon returned and brought the information, that four men on horse back had just passed, who appeared as the forerunners of the main body. The prudent Wallace commanded his men to remain still concealed, while he himself went to obtain more certain intelligence. At length he saw them coming in a dense column, four score and ten gallant soldiers, headed by Sir James Butler, and thanked Heaven, that they were not stronger, and prepared to attack them. The English could not conceive what they were, and were greatly surprised at such an appearance, and could not conjecture their intention, till they approached near, when they perceived the hostile design of Wallace and his warriors. The English brandished their dreadful spears, and rushed upon the

Scots, in the hopes of trampling them under foot, or running them down with their horses. They were boldly and unexpectedly repulsed, and several of their men and horses were slain. Butler alighted from his horse and marshalled his men, in order to defend themselves against a furious enemy. A fierce and sanguinary contest ensued, and a few of the Scots fell under the strong arm of the English captain.—Wallace beheld this omen, became enraged, forced his way through the combating throng, attacked him, and hewed his head in pieces, in presence of his brave warriors. Then wheeling around, laid many of the English on the ground in all directions. Stephen of Ireland and his invincible Scots, also performed their duty and stretched three score of the English on the ground ; the rest fled in confusion to the castle of Kincleven.

The few men who were left as a garrion to defend the place, opened the gate to receive their flying companions ; but Wallace and his men following them so close, entered the same gate with them, seized the castle, shut the gate, drew the bridge, and permitted no one to go out or come in, except according to his pleasure. The women and children he saved, retained them for some days, and then permitted them to depart, with such effects as they chose, to carry along with them. Meantime his men were employed, during five knights, in conveying all the provisions and necessaries which they found in the castle, to the Short-Wood shaws. He then committed the castle to the flames, abandoned it, and wisely retired to the wood for shelter in case of future danger. Lady Butler hastened to Perth, and informed Sir John, her son of the fate of his father, and their misfortunes. Sir John was stung to the heart with grief, and fired with indignation, commanded all the men in Perth and its vicinity, to arms, and repaired to the Short-Wood shaws, in search of the Scots, under the command of William Wallace, of dreaded name and valour.

THE BATTLE OF THE SHORT-WOOD SHAWS.

As soon as the Southerons in St. Johnstown or Perth, heard of the fatal disaster and fall of their garrison at Kincleven, the vowed vengeance on the head of the Scots. Sir John Butler, the son of Sir James Butler of Kincleven, whom Wallace had slain, a valiant chief, was sent with a thousand men of war, to the Short-Wood shaw, to avenge the blood of his father and the other brave men, who died in that awful affray. Butler was impassioned with double rage and spirit of revenge, and poured his men into the shaw in multitudes; archers, spearmen, and swordsmen, with dreadful din of war, resolved to exterminate the little band of Scots, who lodged in the wood. But Wallace heard them approach undismayed, drew up his men in form of battle best calculated to defend themselves,so few in numbers,against a thousandstrong The Southerons advanced in awful front, supposing to cut the Scots to pieces in a few minutes, and a tremendous combat began, the like of it never was seen on the pleasant green banks of the Tay, where such deeds were done, such feats performed, and such glories won, that no human pen can represent, in verse or in prose, arms meeting arms, swords clashing against swords, spears crashing against long claymores, heads and limbs flying asunder, and brains and entrails flowing forth in the presence of the invincible Scots. The Scots were formed into a dense ring, and presented a circular front, like a wall of iron, that nothing could penetrate, nor could a sufficient number of their weaker bodied foes engage to overpower them. As for Wallace, he laboured hard, and often pierced through their ranks, and laid many dead upon the ground, dealing blows of destruction among his enemies. He carefully sought for young Butler through and through the ranks, and at last he eyed him breathing vengeance against his enemy, defended underneath a bowing tree. Intent he mustered all his strength, fiercely struck at Butler, cut down the branch and felled the champion dead on the spot. Loran of Gowrie saw his companion fall dead, under the mighty claymore of Wallace, was enraged and flew at him in a tremendous fury: but Wallace parried off the dreadful blow, and with a sweep of his claymore stretched the younker dead at his feet. Then the valiant Scots fought nobly all that day, and repelled their enemies at every onset, till they in shame withdrew, and left the Scots in possession of the field of battle. Astonishing to tell, that sixty Scots should defeat a thousand Southerons, and only leave seven of their number dead on the field, while full six score of their opponents lay dead around them.—Wallace having won the battle of the Short-Wood shaws, fearing that the enemy would receive reinforcements, and attack them, wearied with the long and desperate contest, withdrew into Methvin wood, and thence retired to Elcho-Park.

WALLACE BETRAYED BY HIS LEMAN IN ST. JOHNSTOWN, AND ESCAPES.

While his invincible warriors remained in Elcho-Park, Wallace was moved with a desire to revisit his sweetheart in the town of Perth; and consequently disguised himself in a friars gown, and proceeded to see the facinating dame! Having spent the night in pleasure, he made a promise to come another day and returned to his men.

In the mean time, the Southerons having obtained information of Wallace's dalliance with the maid, bribed her with gold to betray him into their hands when he returned. According to his promise he returned on the day appointed, incontinent into her chamber of death and danger. Having finished their dalliance, the thought of losing such a trusty, kind and honourable love, struck her with remorse, and she immediately disclosed the nefarious plot to him with weeping, and prayed him to make his escape. He pardoned all her crime with a parting kiss, wiped the tears off her face and forgot the fault of weakness and necessity. He clothed himself in her garments and makes for the gate with all haste and speed. He passed all the watch unsuspected excepting two, who wondered at the amazing size and manly appearance, pursued him until they were out of the reach of the cry of their companions, when Wallace in his Leman's gown, turned round and smote them dead at his feet, hastened to his men, musing on the danger of trusting womankind. He immediately placed his sentinels with orders not to leave their post that night on pain of death; for he well knew that his disappointed enemies would pursue him.

THE BATTLE OF ELCHO-PARK, AND OF TAY.

Kills Faudon; sees his apparation in a dream—proceeds to Lochmaben—wins the castle of Crawford, and slays the captain.

The Southerons being enraged at the escape of Wallace, pursued him with six hundred men, well armed with harness, sword and spear, to beset him in his lurking place in the wood of Elcho. Before them, they sent a famous blood-hound of wondrous scent, to trace the footsteps and hold of Wallace in the woods. Three hundred surrounded the woods, under their captain, Sir Gerard Heron, and three hundred scoured it by the guidance of their blood-hound, under the command of (Sir James) Butler, who landed on Wallace and his brave companions, standing in arms, not one to seven of their enemies.

It was impossible to flee from his surrounding foes. They resolved to conquer or die on the field of battle. The mighty chief unsheathed his conquering claymore, besought the aid of Heaven, and gave the dread command. Fierce he met his invading foes, and dealt his fatal blows like lightning. The tempered edges clashed with horrid din on coats of steel, whence fiery sparkles flashed to brighten the flame of war: but the massy armours and the defensive shields yielded to the nervous arm of matchless Wallace, who, like some awful torrent from a lofty hill, filled all the valley with the wreck of war. He hewed a lane through the martial press, and slew all who dared oppose him. Forty of the enemy lay upon the ground for their temerity; and fifteen of the brave and valiant Scots yielded up their life in defence of their country. The martial hero cut his way through his enemies, rescued all his surviving companions, and escaped towards Tay, in hopes to find a pass, ere his pursuing enemies could overtake them. But alas! no pass could be found, and an infuriated enemy pressed hard upon their rear. "We shall rather die upon the plain, said Wallace, than sink a single drop of Scottish blood in the relentless flood, without revenge: let us stand and be avenged even in our death."

Having heard the breathings of their chieftain, they stood with renewed courage in their own defence. Butler advanced in dread array, bathed in blood, and panting for revenge, and rushed upon the Scots with all his warlike host. Deaths were soon exchanged on every side.—The youthful captain of the noble Scots exerted all his martial fire, run through their ranks and mowed them down like grass, while he himself stood invulnerable in a coat of mail, and raging in his unequal strength. But as he strewed the field with numerous bodies of his enemies, he saw with grief and pain, many of his few companions lying bleeding on the ground, with their shields and good claymores dyed with the blood of their assailants.

Wallace saw no way of relief except in the death of Butler, their captain, whom he keenly sought from place to place through all the throng, and Butler as carefully declined to meet his eye; beneath an aged oak, amidst strong guards he avoided the fatal blow of his claymore. Stephen of Ireland, and faithful Kierly stood firm with Wallace, and dealt their fatal blows on the heads of their surrounding enemies.

Sixty more of the English or Southerons lay dead or weltering in their gore, on the green banks of Tay;

and nine more of the intrepid Scots resigned their breath that day in defence of their liberty. Sixteen now survived to accompany their chief and to flee for their lives, after a day of laborious contests.—They escaped in the night from between two confused parties of Butler's men, unobserved in their flight, and fled to the craggy woods of Dupline.

As they eluded the sight of their enemies, the Southerons sent their blood-hound after them, who quickly traced them out, and brought them in each other's view.

The enemies pursued on fleet coursers; but the Scots depended on their nimble feet. Over two miles of rising ground they had to pass, before they could arrive at any place of strength, or elude the eyes o their numerous enemies. But alas! ill-fated Faudon tired, and would not proceed further, even on the persuasion and help of his faithful companions. Wallace fearing his becoming a traitor as he fell into the hands of his enemies, urged him with words of love, but all in vain. The chieftain became indignant at the designing treachery, reluctantly drew his claymore, and slew the intending traitor. The blood of Faudon stopped the hound and saved the lives of the sixteen survivors. Having despatched the traitor, the rest mounted the rocks like springing deers.

The Southerons having been guided by the slow hound, come to the body of Foudon, and supposed that the Scots had been killing each other.

While they crowded about the dead body of Faudon, Kierley and Stephen of Ireland, mingled among them in the night. Kierley drew his dagger and thrust it into the bosom of Gerard Heron, as he stooped to see the body of Faudon, directing it upwards beneath his armour to his vitals, and laid him dead beside the departed traitor. They cried, " Treason, treason !" in doleful shrieks, being convinced that the audacious claymore of Wallace had pierced the heart of their chieftain. The two brave Scots escaped impending doom, in the midst of the confusion and gloom of the night.

Butler changed colour with grief and rage when he saw Sir Gerard Heron gasping on the ground. He immediately sent some of his men to inter the slain, some to search the woods, some to scour the plain, and others remained with him to guard the passes till the return of day. Wallace, in the mean time, passed through the woods, in grief about the absence of his two brave men, Stephen and Kierly, and arrived safely at Gaskhall, where pressing hunger rendered them bold enough to take two good sheep from a neigbouring fold, and to roast them for supper. There Wallace, in a dream, thought he heard the sound of the loudest horn, and sent all his men, one by one, to learn who should blow the horn of war. None returned to their chieftain, and, as the noise grew louder and louder, his soul was racked with grief and pain about the absence of his companions. The dreadful sound increased in louder roar, and made the warrior tremble. He snatched his dauntless claymore, collected in his strength and moved to the gate, where the frightful appearance of Faudon stood, holding his bleeding head in his hand. Wallace drew a cross and stood, when at that moment, Faudon threw his bloody head at Wallace, who seized it by the hair and returned it to its owner. He awoke and flew out at the window, and fled along the river. Then

Wallace had to wander alone, bewildered in his thoughts and overwhelmed with grief and black ideas revolving in his mind, all the gloomy night. On the return of day Butler awoke, and proceeded to the plains, and there saw poor Wallace laying, sighing and moaning for his companions, demanded his buisness there, with contracted brow, and spurred his fiery horse. Wallace, unmoved, sustained the mighty shock of the furious warrior, and aimed a fatal blow, and cut his enemy to the ground; then he instantly seized and mounted his horse, and scampered along the plains, to evade unequal combat.

A soldier saw his leader fall, and launched his whistling spear at the flying chief, but missed his mark. Yet the enemy intercepted his flight and surrounded the unfortunate chief. Brave Wallace stood, collected all his soul, saw them raging and panting for his blood, drew his dreadful claymore, dealt fate around, swept his bloody way, stretched three warriors dead, and left their chieftain dying on the ground. But the enemy poured in upon him, successive troops, condensed into a crowd, and bend all their united force to bear the chieftain down. The invincible Wallace retires, intrepid and serene, and Parthian like, wounding as he retreated, unsouling twenty of his foes as he withdrew, to adorn the scene of war.

Our glorious warrior, now weak and faint, pursued his gloomy way in dreary wilds, through fens, bogs, and bushes, towards the Forth. But alas! his weary steed sunk to the ground and died upon the plain, and Wallace was compelled to walk on foot without one glimpse of day. He stood on the gloomy banks of the surging flood alone, loosed his massy armour, plunged into it, crossed the stream, and lodged in a thicket, near a widow's house, the following night.

But ere he slept, he despatched two maids, his hostess' two daughters to Gaskhall to search for his beloved companions, and find out their fates.

Next morning, as Wallace repugned the tempta tions of a priest to ensnare him with submission to the power of Edward, Stephen and Kierly arrived in great haste, and rehearsed to their chief all the difficulties which they experienced during his absence. Tears of Joy bedewed the cheeks of those warriors, while they mutually told their adventures and dangers, in the midst of their cruel enemies.

But as Wallace was about to leave that place, the widow came and offered her two sons as volunteers in his service, that they might learn, under his guardianship, the art of war. The mighty chief, with his faithful band of warriors, set out, adorned with horse and arms, for the heath of Dunduff, where brave Sir John Graham held possession under the tyranny of Edward. He had a bold young son, who was endowed by nature and education to excel in war. The good old knight caused his gallant son to swear allegiance to Wallace on his drawn claymore, and to follow him wherever glory and virtue should lead him. Three days Wallace remained in the house of Sir John Graham, and on the fourth he set out with his gallant young pupils to teach them the glorious art of war. He bent his course to his nephew's at Kilbank, that he might collect some warriors, before he should again venture in the field against a powerful and numerous enemy The noble night of Kilbank, his nephew, received every soul as a welcome guest, and enjoyed the love of all.

Meanwhile, the news of the famous deeds of Wallace, and his increasing glory, reached the ears of Piercy, who again attempted to corrupt Sir Ronald Crawford by promises, or to force him by menaces, to influence Wallace to a submission to the government of the usurper; but the mighty chief employed his active thoughts in preparing for war. He dispatched a messenger to Blair and Boyd, to call them to arms in defence of their liberties and their laws.—

The news quickly spread, and all his friends, inured to war and bred to feats of arms, convened in gathering swarms around their chieftain. Wallace was transported with joy and all his cares decreased among such a company of faithful friends, who only waited to receive his commands.

Just as the chief was about to enter on his campaign or expedition against the enemies of his country, he was controlled by the chains of love, that retarded the brilliant course of his warfare. The charming fair lived in Lanerk, very near his native place, Ellerslie, where she was admired by all for the matchless beauties which adorned her person. Wallace beheld the pleasant flame, and can we refuse our Hero the pleasures of nature and desire of his soul A great struggle occupied the mind of Wallace; the love of the fair and the love of his country rolling in his bosom, and he could no longer conceal the pangs of this conflict, " What! shall I give up my heart to love and destroy all my future schemes of war; shall I thus lose myself in pleasant dreams, while Scotland claims my bosom! No, I stifle this inglorious flame, and erase her image from my remembrance; rise glory rise! assume thy wonted charms, carry me into thine arms, and drown each thought in the loud alarms of war; my duty and my country call me hence, adieu, fair Marion, adieu." As the love-struck hero moved away, a maid arrived from his lovely fair with an invitation to visit her habitation. "Marion sends her compliments and would be glad to behold the bravest son of his country." The chief was amazed and cried impatiently, "I go," and proceeded through a secret back path to her house. There the lovely pair regaled themselves with a sweet converse, and concluded the match.

"But his duty called him to the field,
And love to conquest now must yield,
"Sweet maid," he cried, "again "I'll come to thee,
When the loud trumpet sounds to victory."

He urged his course to Lochmaben, where his enemy, full grown in arrogance and glorying in power, Clifford, the inhuman youth commanded, and vaunted in his inhuman conquests over the land.—Wallace had scarce reached the devoted town when Clifford began to brand the Scots with contumelies. He pursued the haughty lord, pierced his heart with his awful claymore, and left the town to warn his faithful friends of the expected enemy; who immediately on the death of their chief pursued them. The enemy appeared in burnished arms, and shot their arrows with certain speed and aim and wounded John Blair, his worthy chaplain. Wallace saw him bleed and turned in awful rage to meet his foes. Having ordered an attack, his little band rushed upon their enemies and received their adverse shock ; none of either side dare seek a base retreat, until the English army was thinned with numerous slain, and the whole field covered with multitudes of dead. Yet still their new troops advanced in thickening crowds, which covered the fields around with the clangor of war.— Moreland too, the flower of arms, moved to the field with lightning in his eyes ; his armour yielded blazing splendour, his plume nodded from a distance, and increased the tide of war ; martial terror gloomed upon his brows as his boiling rage glowed in his heaving bosom.

Keen in arms the mighty chief meditated the ruin of the Scots, and his very appearance seemed to raise the hopes of the Southeron's, as it swelled the tide of war. The dauntless Scots could not even attempt to flee, they were closely wedged on every side, and fully resolved to win or die. Both sides assaulted, and vied each other in tremendous feats, thickened the combat, and thinned the field. Wallace rode thundering through the tempest of the conflict, distinguished by the orby shield, and sought the dreaded Moreland. His glancing eye caught the raging chief, and at him aimed the ponderous blade, which cut his neck in two, and severed his head from his body. Wallace then seized his horse and wheeled around to revive the thunder of the war. The chieftain of the Scots, as if inspired by heaven with more than human might, inclined the scale of fight to victory with his own arm. Heaps on heaps expired on every side, and all the verdant grass was dyed with human gore. At last the Southerons lost their courage on the death of their champion, and fled to the castle, where fierce

Gravestock reigned in abandoned pride and ease, deriding all their terrors and scorning all their fears.

As soon as fierce Gravestock perceived the defeat and death of Moreland, he commanded all his men in arms to issue forth to the field, and meet the approaching Scots. He again revived the tempest of war; while Wallace had withdrawn from the bloody scene of victory to rest his wearied limbs. But he soon returned to his brave companions, and determined the fate of the day. The Southerons saw him rise, like a lion in his full strength casting an iron glare, and cursed the fearful sight. "Oh, don't, they cried, anticipate our doom! return, return; don't brave the impending fate! yonder he comes; behold the godlike chieftain, whose mighty arm alone sweeps the field!" "Ha! ye dastards! cried Gravestock, their intrepid General, with a frown of rage, and spurred his horse, his strength owes its being to your fears alone."

Wallace's horse sunk under him, and his rider being overcome by fatigue, could not tempt the rising tumult of the roaring war, which rolled along in fierce encounters. Meantime, immortal Graham, as if despatched by Heaven, advanced with a brave retinue of warriors. He joined the battle and raised the clamorous shouts and cries through all the field. Graham rushed through the war and swept the standing field, as if some fierce tide, bounding in the thickest, of the fight. Wallace, on foot, cuts his bloody path, and braving death, he stems the flood of war; he fights in wearied ardour, besmeared with blood and dust, and reaped the field, where dread and fate appeared to mow his intrepid followers. Thus all his brave companions urged the course and repulsed their foes in foul disgrace.

The champion from the front of battle retreats, and Wallace urged the chase, as if he gained new strength to cut their chieftain down; but swift Graham, quick as lightning, vied with his noble leader, and swept the rabble down. "Away, cried Wallace, why disgrace thy sword? fly at yon fleeing chief and reap a nobler field:" and as the youthful heroes shot along the ranks in rapid haste, the new fired Graham sought Gravestock retreating off the field. The mighty Scot raised his claymore, as lightning in the air, and clave his monstrous head. No force could impede its descending motion, nor prevent the yawning chasm that effused his gushing soul.

Wallace, meanwhile, strewed the bloody ground with corses of the dead, and finished the burning chase.

The brave warriors now meet, and unite with kind intercourse of souls, each pleased with the view of his victorious friends panting after a well fought day.—All the victors headed by Wallace, sat down at night to meditate new toils of war, among the heaps of slain; and ere morning directed their march to Lochmaben, to explore the town in the shades of night.

As they approached the gate, they found the keeper watching alone, and aimed a random blow, and laid him dead in silence. His following band advanced in haste, and surprised the house, whence clamour, shrieks and cries issued to rend the skies; naught but groans of wretches resounded through all the apartments of the fortress, where mirth and pride had reigned.

The victors, now wearied with toils of war, gladly reclined to satiate the calls of nature, on the spoils of their opulent enemies. The sated warriors left the humble town, and bent their rapid course toward the flowing Clyde, to repose in sleep their exhausted limbs. The god of sleep soon embraced them in the retired vale, and eased them of the bloody toils of day. The restless warrior dreamed of an unsubdued fortress where the enemies triumphed, and ere it was day they were awoke with the sound of the martial horn of their chieftain : all determined to level its proud walls with the ground, before they could return to rest.

Wallace, in front, advanced with eager speed towards the devoted town, where their enemies wallowed in luxuries and raised their drunken mirth.—The enraged chief gave the dreadful order to assail the gates, to guard the passes and invest the fortress with united force. The eager warriors combined their powers and rushed upon their foes. Wallace sought the house, where the sottish captain sat, and hurled him headlong to the shades of night. His men, with vieing rage, mingled their blood with their feast, and their bodies lay in grinning death, and weltering in their gore.

Graham, meantime, scaled the piles of the fort, plied his hands to fling the brands, in order to consume the lofty roof, which soon descended in volumes of fire to scorch their trembling foes. Ah! what shrieks within and yellings of despair, blended with the horror, to consummate the fiery death. The roof, turret, and all around, tumbled to the ground like a burst of thunder, and crushed the wretches underneath its burning columns. Thus the great fortress appeared, on the dawn of day, in heaps of smoking ruins, and half burnt bodies of their fallen enemies, lying in piles of ashes ! ! !

WALLACE RETURNS TO LANERK,

Marries Marion—removes her from the seat of war goes to fight against Hesilrig and Thorn.

The conquering hero, having swept the country of his numerous foes in many brilliant victories, returned in guise to Lanerk, to espouse his loving Marion, and to refresh his sense with the social pleasures of connubial nature. Moved with the soft flame of love to see his lovely Marion, he forgot the danger of his enemies' being posted in the bosom of his country, being resolved to wed his intended spouse and consummate the future days of his life with the joys of hymen.

The happy pair did not long enjoy the connubial blessings of peace and sweet intercourse together in Lanerk; for while he remained with his Marion during the months of April, May and June, the Southerons gained ground, and re-occupied all the principal towns and forts of the country, and the martial soul of Wallace was roused, and he could no longer restrain the fire that burned in his heart, to rescue his country from the tyranny of a cruel usurper. Love and honour alternately ruled his passions for some time, and he anxiously staid with Marion ; but the love of his country and of glory, at length overcame all the love of his beloved consort, and he again sets out to vindicate the rights of Scotland.

But, oh! what a parting was realized on that solemn occasion! can any one depict the strength and purity of the love of those two benign bosoms, when the youthful Wallace parted with his Marion, his loving, beautiful, young spouse, to head the Scottish warriors! can prose or poesy paint the motions of their united souls on that day, when this faithful pair expressed their grief to each other, and soothed the passions of each other's breast; he desirous to carry his wife beyond the hazards of war, she imploring him to take her along with him, mutually wishing security from the cruel rapine and plunder of their oppressors, who raged in lusts and wallowed in spoils.

" Will you go, said Marion, will you go where the alarms of war call you, and where battles rage, and leave me exposed to every wilful enemy? See Hesilrig appears in lustful rage, he will deride my passions and insult my fears; he shows no mercy nor quarter: I shall sink beneath the blow of this cruel warrior. The wife of Wallace cannot be long concealed, and I shall die in your absence. Oh! take me with you! whatever shoul happen to us, I am willing to live or die with thee."

" Cease, cease, to grieve, said Wallace. Oh, Marion! If just Heaven has ordained my safe return, I shall see you again, and if He has otherwise deter mined, He will protect you, or carry you into the mansions of bliss."

A long and moving colloquy ensued between them and continued with equal conflict until the break of day. when young Wallace went out to the fields, implored the aid of Heaven on his arduous undertaking, blew his martial horn, and assembled his followers to go out to the fields of victory.

The English soon perceived their danger, and observed the progress of the war, and prepared for fierce encounter under the command of Hesilrig and Thorn. One thousand strong; all savage warriors, armed with swords, spears, and javelins, made head against the Scots, and a sanguinary combat ensued. Stern vengeance frowned on the brows of the warriors, and fired by different passions, the two nations joined in battle. The guilty invaders armed with pride and ambition, the patriotic Scots boldly attempted to check the tyrant's reign, and maintain their freedom. All the plains were soon covered with arms, and the countless arrows flew from well stored quivers, until the Scots being overpowered with numbers, withdrew in the silence of the night, to Cartline Craigs, in order to save his little band of heroes, and to wait impatiently the rise of day.

In that solemn night, the cruel Hesilrig having heard that Marion had concealed Wallace, proceeds to the residence of innocent Marion, and demands of her, information of the lurking place of Wallace, her beloved husband. He threatened her with instant death if she did not reveal his secret abode. The trembling young Marion shed tears of fear and sorrow in vain, while his huge sword waved around her head, and menaced her immediate destruction. The cowardly Hesilrig disregarded her prayers and her tears, abjured all ties of honour, and relentlessly plunged his ruthless sword into her heaving bosom!!! Alas! Marion sunk beneath the traitor's sword, the sword of a disappointed lover, and the pale hand of death sealed up her closing eyes! Alas for Marion! stretched on the cold ground, and her offspring doomed never to see the light of day! Alas for pregnant Marion, cruelly murdered by the enemy of her husband and her country, and her promising race concealed forever in nature's womb.

Quick as on the wings of the wind, the unhappy news reached the ears of loving Wallace, and chilled his heart with the dismal catastrophe of his dear Marion. All his warriors sympathized in tears of sorrow; Graham with all his mourning band could not withstand the shock; but Wallace beheld their tears and bade them cease to weep for departed Marion. "Why all this waste of tears, cried the noble Wallace; will they recall her fleeting shade? Let tears give way to nobler toils of war, and swords perform in strictest justice, what words would express Hear me, O brave Graham, thou companion of my arms! to thee I swear, that this claymore shall not be sheathed till I revenge the death of my dearest, dearest Marion! Heavens! what toils of death and war, rivers of floating blood, and hills of slain, shall mark our course; and for her sake ten thousand shall welter on the plain."

While thus the chieftain spoke, his melancholy troops gazed on him to catch the sound of war with pleasing anguish. Fierce vengeance steeled every warrior's heart, martial fire bent every bow, and passion nerved every hand of those true hearted Scots "Come, says the chief, to yonder Lanerk let us wing our course in the silence of the night, and let us surprise those murderers in their sleep, that ven geance may overtake them : justice requires blood for blood."

They obeyed his commahd and marched to Lanerk, and ere it was day, entered the devoted town, where the English lay in perfect security. Wallace divided his men into two hostile bands and pointed out the places of attack ; the one to storm the castle where Hesilrig lay, and the other under the command of Sir John Graham to burn down their dwellings. To Hesilrig's chamber Wallace winged his intended course. He threw a huge stone on the gate and broke the bars, bolts, and brazen hinges, entered Hesilrig's apartment, surprised him in the dead of night, and hurled him headlong to the shades of death, as he stood trembling, and saw the injured man advance, holding his huge claymore in his hand, and uttering words of inexorible vengeance. "And thou thoughtest, traitor, the fiere hero cried, that I would be remiss, or unable to resent the cruel injury done to me and the Scots, in spilling the precious blood of Marion." As thus he spoke he raised his claymore and swung the ponderous steel on his head. The felon sunk to the ground and breathed out his guilty soul.

Meantime, Sir John Graham commands his men to throw fire-brands on the roofs and guard the passes. Thorn saw, in dire amazement, the ruinous blaze that was to embrace him and his followers in the arms of death, but could not avert his doom.

On the dawn of morning, the victors saw the heaps of slain, and many half-burned bodies of their enemies, in piles of smoking ruins. "Enough, cried Sir John Graham, enough, Wallace ; Albion's ensign is freed, and glitters in the wind ; Scotia is redeemed with heaps of dead." But the hero naa no sooner won one victory than he bent his way to some more glorious field, reserved for the plains of Biggar.

THE BATTLE OF BIGGAR.

Wallace had no sooner avenged the blood of deai Marion on the head of Hesilrig and his guilty crew in unhappy Lanerk, the death place of the fair and beautiful Marion Braidfoot, heiress of Lammington, than he quickly leads his victorious bands to the plains of Biggar. There he saw, while his men lay encamped on a rising ground, his numerous enemies stretched out in wide array along the plain, and his heart biggened with the glorious sight, as if some scene of victory had presented to his view.

In the morning watch, every soldier roused with the sound of the clarion eagerly seized his ready shield, drew his broad claymore, and strode along the field in a dense column, to meet their assailants. From right to left, the wings extended, condensed, and closed to the thickening combat.

As the soldiers thus were gathered into martial clouds, with hearts beating high, waiting the least command, and death stood lingering in their lifted hands; Wallace viewed with a skilful eye the weakness of his enemies, saw with joy the impassioned aspect of his men, and thus addresed them :

" To day, my friends, let us fight the battle of our country ; let us hazard unequal fight, in the cause ot our wives and our children ; let our claymores be deeply drenched in the blood of the enemies and oppressors of Scotland, and then our toils will soon be over in glorious victory. Around our heads, guardian angels stand to guide the javelins in our hands, and to direct our claymores to Edward's heart. Let glorious liberty inspire our souls ; let injuries steel our hearts ; and let cruel Edward's tent be our mark in this impending combat."

As thus he spoke, the love of glory fired every heart, and the love of liberty armed every soul, and quick as lightning the Scots legion descended the brow of the hill to attack their foes marshalled on the plain. The enemies saw them descend in torrents, rushing in massy steel to meet them, in closest ranks, and were surprised at the swiftness of the descending war.

The Scots received the first onset of their numerous enemies in the form of a circle, which seemed as impenetrable as a wall of iron, and then urged their way towards the monarch's tent. There was the dreadful conflict of warriors, there a thousand lay bleeding on the plain ; swords, shields, claymores and spears, lay mingled in confusion, and the field was reaped by the Scots on that awful day. The orby shield of Wallace was distinguished from a distance to tempest the field, and floated in the midst of the throng. Imperious death attended his claymore, and certain doom was designed for the usurper. But fierce Kent employed his dreadful spear in another part of the contest, and destroyed as many of the Scots. On his bounding courser he bore away his lord over heaps of dead, and the little band of Scots could scarcely withstand the mighty sweep of the hand of that invader.

Wallace saw his men retreat on his approach, hasted in fury to the fainting squadron, heaved his orby shield, resolved in arms to meet the dreaded enemy, and spread destruction all around him, in equal conflict. The battle lasted long, and the fortune of the day hung long uncertain in furious suspense. But at length, Wallace mustering all his strength, forced his bloody way, and smote fierce Kent, and stretched him lifeless on the ground. Then the king fled from the field, and the Scots pursued him till the going down of the sun, when the Caledonian victors regaled themselves with the wine and spoils of the enemy's camp.

Longcastle saw with grief the foul retreat of his men, attempted to rally, and encourage them to return upon the Scots in the dead of the night, and to surprise them while they lay drunk with the wine of their camp. "Whence does our hearts feel this coward terror, defeat never stained our conquering arms, said Longcastle, stay, take courage; why ignobly flee? bravely conquer or bravely die. We can easily vanquish yon handful of Scots now absorbed in luxury." Then Longcastle gave the command and led them to the fight, in hopes to surprise the Scots, under the darkness of the night. But the alert Scottish watchmen descried their rallying enemies, and quickly informed Wallace their chieftain, who as a lion in full strength, arose, blew the clarion to arms, and summoned all his warriors to battle.

At this critical moment, a deep morass divided the two armies. They eagerly view each other, and martial passions impassioned either host. The English Duke was unable to restrain his fury, encouraged his troops, and ventured to tread the faithless ground on his fiery steed. All plunged at once into the morass and thousands sunk to rise no more. Those who struggled to the other side, only met a change of death; the fiery Scots soon deprived them of breath.

Longcastle gained the dry ground and stood upon the shoal. Graham saw him, raised his claymore, and received the rising enemy. Back sunk the courser and overlaid his lordly rider. Thus proud Edward lost the important day, and to his kingdom led his host away.

Thus Wallace, having returned thanks to propitious Heaven, proceeded to reduce the castle of Dumbarton, which was situated on a rock on the banks of the rapid rolling Cree. They marched all that day, and reposed themselves in the evening, but ere it was day, Wallace sounded the clarion, disposed his troops under brave Kierly and himself, and in the silence of the gloomy night, strained up the steep rock, slew the centinel as he lay sleeping at the eastern gate, entered the castle, and dispatched every opponent. All gave way; some leaped over the walls, and tumbled down the steep and sunk into the deep below; others bravely attempted to repel their assailants and met their fate under the hewing sweep of the Scottish claymores. Ten thousand cries seemed to rend the sky, from their confused enemies: cries of mercy and cries of revenge mingled in their crowd, amidst yells and groans of fallen warriors, while the slogans of "Wallace and Freedom," "Scotland and Liberty," re-echoed from the Scottish lines to seal the impending doom of their enemies.

Thus sunk the strength of the proud Southerons in the strong hold of Dumbarton, and thus fell the oppressors of Scotland.

The English then sued for peace, and agreed to ratify the treaty of Ruthington vesa, at Ruthenglen, church for one year in February, 1297, in order to have time to recruit their strength, and again attempt the conquest of the country.

HOSTILITIES RECOMMENCED.

Wallace burns the barns of Ayre, drives Bishop Beck from Glasgow, and kills Lord Piercy.

Good Wallace thus concluded a truce for one whole year with his treacherous enemies ; but ere one month had elapsed, they plotted the ruin of the Scottish warriors, and determined, by awful murder, to enchain the country.

The King of England proceeded to Scotland and held a council at Carlisle, of his captains, in June, 1297. No Scot was there except the traitor, Sir Aymer de Vallance, who had deserted their cause in former times. In this council they consulted how they might cut off all the Barons of Ayre, and thereby involve the invincible Wallace in the general massacre.

Sir Amyer de Vallance, deeply versed in the mysteries of Pluto, proposed a scheme to ensnare the chiefs of Scotland, and involve their lives ; a plot which hell could never have contrived ; an advice, which belzebub could not have given, that will ever stamp the character of consenting Southerons with everlasting infamy. He advised them to appropriate the four barns of Ayre for a *Justice Ayre* or general council of the Scottish Barons, to call them all to it, under the pretence of settling the affairs of the nation on receiving a schedule of their estates, that quiet possession might be granted them under the great seal of Lord Aymer de Vallance, the Deputy Warden o' Scotland, who had just arrived at Ayre, and there to despatch them as they entered one by one, into the barns.

Lord Arnulf, a cruel and bloody justice to whom Hell could not produce a match, undertook to dispatch the Scottish Nobles, in the bloody Barns of Ayre. Sir Ronald Crawford went to Ayre, and dreading no harm entered the Barns, where the pretended Council sat; and on the 18th of June 1297, was immediately hoisted up to a Baulk.

The Wallaces, Crawfords, Kennedys, Blairs, Montgomeries, Campbells, Barclays, Boyds, Stewarts, and many other brave Barons of Scotland had the same fate in those sanguinary Barns of Ayre, and their massacred bodies were piled up in heaps in the cor ners of those slaughter houses. The way and manner in which the Southerons executed this horrid deed were by placing strong men to keep the entry, to allow one only to enter at a time, to slip a running cord over each of their heads as they entered singly, and by placing men in another part of the barn to haul the rope the moment it snared its victim, whose carcass was successively thrown into the opposite corner! great numbers, even eighteen score of Nobles and landed men entered, none came out alive! many noble warriors and heroes were betrayed and hanged on that day of mourning! such forms of massacre was never invented before in any nation under the canopy of weeping Heaven; such a deed was never heard of in the world! and to crown their sanguinary barbarity, all their bodies as naked as they were born, were cast out in heaps to the public view, and exposed in black derision! Ah! dreadful work of man! kind Heaven! shall our hosts now sleep? while our old men, women and children chaunt their coronachs over the bodies of the massacred Chiefs! shall our country endure such cruel massacre of her sons without resisting the injury? No; good Robert Boyd assembled twenty men of Wallace's party, and commanded them in his absence. Kierley, Cleland, Stephen of Ireland and others fled to Longlandwood, with sorrowful hearts, after they had appointed a good woman, his old nurse Elspa, to inform Wallace of the treachery and massacre in the bloody Barns of Ayre, as soon as he should arrive in town, so that he might escape the snare laid for him by the cruel Southerons.

Wallace hastened to Ayre, and, as he passed along, the woman loudly called him, and said, "Nothing but breach of faith are within these walls, our Barons and Knights were hanged like beasts to a tree as they entered the Barns." Wallace wept for the loss of his dear relations, the Wallaces and Crawfords, and asked her, whether his uncle Sir Ronald Crawford was butchered there. "Yes," said the faithful matron, "I saw him cast out dead and naked, I kissed his pale lips, covered his boby with a cloth, and wept. Thou art his sister's son, revenge his death

I pray thee, with all thy might and haste; I shall assist you, as much as a woman can do in the case of retributive justice." Then he enquired of her of Robert Boyd, William Crawford, Adam Wallace, &c. anu scampered off to Longlandwood and mourned for his dear friends.

Meantime Lord Arnulf sent fifteen well harnessed Englishmen and a Macer to bring him back to law. They rode furiously to Wallace, who turned upon them with his broad claymore in his hand. The first of his numerous enemies he cut asunder through the middle; the next received a fatal blow; the third he clave down through the body; the fourth he levelled to the ground; and the fifth he felled dead on the spot. Three men who were with him killed another five of the enemy, and the rest fled to tell their lord how ten men out of fifteen were killed by four Scots, concluding that all would have shared the same fate, if their horses had not carried them away in full speed, and that the Scots were so fierce and strong, that every stroke laid one of them dead on the field.

The Southerons all concluded that Wallace must have been in that encounter, and a Knight answered, "if Wallace hath escaped this justice Ayre, then all that we have done is in vain." Arnulf replied, "what would ye do if there were many enemies, when you seem to be frightened at one man, and although he was there I would count the matter light, who stays here shall be a Knight in these realms, and I shall deal out the lands of Scots dispatched yesterday, to true Englishmen in the morning."

The Southerons all repaired to their quarters.—Four thousand men lodged in the town and Barns of

Ayre that night, after they had gorged themselves with plenty of meat, wine and ale. Supposing no danger from the Scots, they placed no sentinels at the gates, fell into a profound sleep, by the bumpers they had taken, after the labours and toils of that bloody day in the Barns, and were laying in security.

As soon as the faithful matron saw them laying in this unguarded state, she ran with some men to Longlandwood, to inform Wallace of their drunken and naked condition. "Yon bloodhounds, she said, are all drunken and could not see a Scotsman in their company." "If that be true," answered Wallace, "its time to move and set a fire unto their dwellings." Three hundred choice men by this time had rallied round his standard, willing and ready to spend the last drop of their blood "for Wallace and Freedom." Wallace called a council of war and consulted with them what course they should take to be avenged of the deaths of their nobles and relations. They first cast lots between five of their company, viz. William Wallace, Boyd, Crawford, Adam Wallace and Auchinleck, appealing to the court of Heaven to decide who should be their Commander in the attack which they meditated.—The lot fell on William Wallace, even the third time. He then rose, and drawing his sword, solemnly vowed to the Almighty Disposer of Events, that he should be avenged on their cruel oppressors, for the death of his kindred Scots, whose blood was shed in the Barns of Ayre. "I shall make them all pass through the flames, before I either eat, drink or sleep," said the Chieftain, and he kept his vow.

The faithful matron chalked all the doors where the English lay; Wallace sent twenty men to fasten all their doors with osiers; sent fifty more to lie in ambush at the gates of the castle, to kill all who might attempt to escape, and the rest he commanded to sur round the Barns, and not to allow a Southeron to escape on pain of death. The women brought fire and flax, and all combustibles to them, and the soldiers set fire to their houses and the Barns and raised a huge conflagration over the heads of his mortal enemies. Wallace then called out to Lord Arnulf, "execute your law against us who live and have escaped your judgment, deal not our land, for faith that is not fair, thy cruel bloodshed confess and mourn, take now thy choice whether to hang or burn." None escaped this fiery ruin, lord or night, and all were burned or buried in the smoking ruins. When the huge roofs fell in among them, O what an awful and lamentable noise of shrieks and groans of consuming warriors. Some sought the doors and were cut down by the surrounding Scots, or driven back into the fire, to learn to be hangmen there.

Friar Drumlaw, Prior of Ayre, had seven score of men lodged upon him that night. As soon as he found them to be all asleep, he caused seven of his brother Friars, to command the English armour and choose their swords, and led them from house to house where the Southerons lay, and dispatched them in their sleep. Five thousand died that night by fire and sword. O what a night of justest vengeance was that in which the Castle and Barns of Ayre were burned!

Wallace and his men assembled after the burning of the English garrison, and he said to them, "You know, my friends, that Justice Court was also appointed for Clydesmen at Glasgow, in presence of

Bishop Beck and Lord Piercy, let us wing our course towards that town and surprise our enemies who have murdered our kindred." He left the Burgesses to watch the house of Ayre with vigilance, and having refreshed themselves he ordered their march to Glasgow on the choicest of English horses, now all cavalry, three hundred strong, to attack their ruthless enemies. They passed the Bridge of Glasgow, before their enemies knew of their coming; but Lord Piercy mustered his men in good order and prepared for a fierce contest with the Scots' warrior, Bishop Beck and Piercy led a thousand men in bright armour to the approaching combat. Wallace advanced in head of his men and reconnoitred his enemies, and returned with the grand plan of the attack in his mind. He divided his men into two squadrons, harnessed them and called true Auchinleck, saying, "Uncle, before we attack these adversaries, I ask you whether you will attack them in the rear or tail, or gallop up in front, kneel down and receive the Prelate's benison." "I will not be ambitious, quoth Auchinleck, yourself may take his blessing for me. That is the post of honour, and your right, I shall bear up his tail with all my might." "Since we must part, it will be wrong to stay too long from us, said Wallace, your men must not regard their numbers. March on your squadron fast, for God's sake, elude the view of the Southerons in marching round to the rear through the north-east raw." Adam Wallace, and Auchinleck marched briskly with seven score of men up the back part of the town, and Wallace and Boyd with two hundred and sixty men galloped up in sight of the enemy, along the plain street.

The English wondered how there were so few of them, and an ensign of Beck and Piercy demanded of them what they were, when a fierce encounter immediately commenced with dreadful din on either side. The hardy Scots bravely fought and heaped the streets with slain enemies. They peirced their plates with their claymores and brought them down at every blow. The dust rose like smoke around the combatants, darkened the sun, and ascended to the clouds.

Lord Piercy's men were expert warriors and fought most valiantly with Wallace and Boyd for some time, but in good time, Adam Wallace and brave Auchinleck boldly rushed upon the rear of the enemy, with broad claymores, and galled them severely. The Southerons faced about and received the Scots warmly, but the Scots in front and rear, made such slaps or chasms among the ranks of their enemies as never yet had been seen in any fight.

The Scottish claymores swept the field, and Wallace amidst the throng, swung his long and heavy claymore, and at Piercy aimed a dreadful blow and clave his head in pieces, and Bishop Beck saw his men fail and led them off in confusion through a wood and marched them off to Bothwell.

The English left seven hundred dead on the field of battle. Then Wallace pursued the fugitives to Bothwell; but Aymer de Vallance, escaped in flight from that tremendous contest and defeat.

The followers of Sir William Wallace soon acquired the form of an army, after such signal victories, and many of the nobles of Scotland; joined him. Among others, Robert, Bishop of Glasgow ; Robert Bruce, Earl of Carrick ; James Stewart, Lord Steward of Scotland ; Sir John Stewart, his brother ; Sir Andrew Murray, of Bothwell ; Sir William Douglass, of Glasgow ; Robert Boyd ; Lord Campbell, of Argyle ; Richard Lundie, &c. To defeat their attempts to liberate themselves from tyranny, Edward sent an army of 40,000 men to suppress them.

The Scots met them at Irvine, protected by a lake in front and entrenchments on the flanks. This little band was under the command of four Captains. equal in power over their divisions; Bishop of Glasgow, William Douglass, Andrew Murray and William Wallace for they were not yet disposed to confer the chief command on Wallace, and they became so divided in their sentiments, that they accommodated matters with the enemy, on receiving an indemnity for all past offences. The treacherous Southerons, however, broke the agreement, confined the Bishop to Roxburgh Castle, and Sir William Douglass to the Castle of Berwick.

But the brave soul of Wallace could never permit him to compromise with the English, he only despised to quarrel with the other captains who were of higher rank, and prudently withdrew with all his voluntary band and fell upon the rear of the English army, retreating through Galloway took three hundred men and their baggage. Wallace then retired to Dunduff to refresh his men, and remained with good Sir John Graham five days, in the summer season, telling him all that had befallen them in Ayre and Glasgow, even until he received tidings from some true-hearted Scots, that Buchan, Athol, Monteith and Lorn had marshalled all their forces against faithful Argyle, in the cause of the usurper Edward. Campbell, of Argyle, kept his heritage of Lochlow, in spite of Edward's power and the bloody sword of Macfadzean, who was promised the possession of Argyle, &c. on event of their conquest. Edward promised the lands of Lorn to John, in case of the dispossession of Duncan the lawful proprietor of the lands. In hopes to acquire great possessions, even of five Lordships, Macfadzean mustered an army of vile runnagates consisting of fifteen thousand malefactors and exiles, mostly from Ireland, who spared neither man, woman nor child in their march through the devoted villages and districts of Caledonia, "Burn, Destroy and Kill," were the constant commands of that sanguinary Macfadzean.

As soon as Campbell understood, that Macfadzean entered Lochlow, he placed three hundred men in Craigmuir and held that place of strength against all the powers of Edward and the army of Macfadzean. He broke down the bridge across the river Forth, and defended the ford that none should pass over at any place, except at a narrow place, between two rocks where four men could not pass over in front, Macfadzean attempted to pass. At this juncture, Duncan of Lorn went off in quest of Wallace to succour the men of Argyle against the merciless host of Macfadzean.

Gilmichael, a brave footman, accompanied Duncan to guide him in the way to Wallace, Earl Malcom, hostess to Wallace, with his brave men and

Sir John Graham and Richard of Lundie, assembled their several forces, marched with him, and disputed the field against bloody Macfadzean and his merciless crew.

WALLACE KILLS MACFADZEAN.

Wallace then marched to view the savage host of Macfadzean, low, posted in Lochlow, passed to the north of Stirling Castle where the cruel Ruickby commanded in the service of Edward. Wallace looked back to Earl Malcom and said, "what would you think of reducing this fortress by some stratagem, and clear the country behind us of these oppressors." Sir John Graham immediately agreed with him in the propriety of the undertaking, and he divided his men so that the English could not discover their strength ; placed Earl Malcom to lie in ambush, while he and Sir John Graham, with one hundred brave Scots warriors rode through the town in noble order, passed the Castle and made towards the bridge. Ruickby saw them with great impatience, and caused seven score of archers to sally forth, pursue and engage them ; but Wallace never felt fear and slew the foremost with his spear. Sir John Graham also transfixed the first he met ; but broke his spear into the second in front. Then he drew his gallant claymore to receive a host of archers which crowded on him and killed his horse.

Wallace saw the jeopardy of good Sir John Graham, fighting on foot, lighted from his horse, with some other brave men in armour, and repulsed their numerous enemies, which had hoped to escape into the Castle. But noble Earl Malcom started from his ambush and marched his men between them and the Castle, and then made tremendous havoc among their surrounded enemies.

Many English nobles fell that day, and the Scots chieftain winged his course towards Ruickby, and severed his head from his shoulders with one sweep of his claymore. His two sons and 30 men escaped and re-entered the Castle.

The Lennox men would not leave the Castle, but besieged it with great vigilance, while Wallace proceeds to meet cruel Macfadzean, against whom he had sworn revenge, vowing that he would never sleep sound nor rest contented, till he should dispatch that wicked tyrant and murderer of our men, women and children. Two thousand brave and valiant Scots warriors assembled to Wallace at Stirling bridge and rode with him to Argyle, under the guidance of Duncan of Lorn.

Meantime Ruickby's sons concluded to capitulate to the noble Earl Malcom, on condition that he would spare their lives and let them return to their native land. Wallace still continues his march, with all his force to encounter Macfadzean, foot and horse, by the direction of Gilmichael, the spy, whom Duncan of Lorn had sent to lead them to the ranks of the enemy. But his men began to faint in their forced marches, a little beyond Strathsillon, and he left the feebler men to follow the rest of the army as they were able to accomplish the journey.

Wallace then divided his men, numbered five hundred stout Westland men to fight under himself; five hundred to fight under Sir John Graham; five hun dred to fight under Lundie, the captains of their several hosts; and five hundred had loitered behind.—They marched over a high mountain into Gendoher, met their spy and Lord Campbell, with three hundred valiant, chosen men, and mutually encouraged each other never to dread their foes, who were then half naked and almost destitute of arms.

Then to Lochdocher they marched with a design to surprise their enemy. An out-spy and Gilmichael seized on his person, and brought him into the posses sion of the Scots, and he never returned to tell Mac fadzean the news.

The men are now forced to alight and to turn their horses loose, and Wallace cried, "let us see who walks best on foot, and traverse mosses, moors, craigs and woods." So along the banks of the river, three in front, he led his men, until all had passed up the craggy mountains, eighteen hundred brave Scots, and surprised Macfadzean and his numerous host in front, and drove them with great havoc into confusion. They soon rallied again, and collecting all their banditti strength, they rushed upon the val iant Scots, who received them with their dreadful claymores, repulsed them and drove them back more than five acres breadth with great slaughter.

Wallace made a space of the reaped field about a rood of land, and Sir John Campbell, Lundie, Adam

Wallace and Robert Boyd signalized themselves in the sanguinary contest, and as Captains of the Scots, encouraged their brave men, in the front of the battle. The conflict lasted for two hours, and seemed long to hang in some uncertainty of success on either side, until the Scots chiefs condensed their warriors and pressed forwards in dense columns, making fearful chasms in the Irish ranks under cruel Macfadzean, and drove them over craggy rocks, into the flood below, where two thousand sunk to rise no more.

The Scots under Macfadzean laid down their arms, and on their knees loudly cried for mercy and quarter. "They are our own blood, said Wallace, we are bound to give penitents generous quarters, but these foreign murderers of our men, women and children, deserve no mercy; blood calls for blood." But Macfadzean escaped with fifty men to a stone cave under Craigmuir. Duncan of Lorn desired permission of Wallace to go with a detachment of brave men to visit the cave, who, when they arrived killed the fifty men and brought the head of Macfadzean on a spear Lord Campbell placed the bloody head of Macfadzean on lofty Craigmuir, in honour of Ireland.

THE VIRTUOUS SCOTS SWORE FIDELITY TO WALLACE.

In a Council at Ardchatton proclaimed him Regent or Warden of Scotland, or Viceroy in Bruce's absence. Restores Duncan to his heritage of Lorn.

Wallace took Stirling Castle; recovered Argyle and Lorn, Perth, Cooper of Angus, and Glames, demolished the Castle of Forfar, Brichinhin and Montrose, surprised Dunnoter and garrisoned it, entered Aberdeen while in flames, and proceeded to besiege the Castle of Dundee.

Wallace accepted of the names and titles of Regent, not out of ambition or desire to rule, but because it was a title of honour and great responsibility conferred on him by his countrymen out of their pure love and benevolence. In this office he behaved so valiantly, that in a short time, by a brave army of true hearted Scots, he recovered all the places of strength in the kingdom, and reduced the bordermen on the south of Scotland to peace and oroer.

They flocked to Wallace from all parts of the land and acknowledged the victorious hero as Warden, and he governed the kingdom with great honour and strict justice and mercy, and fought the battles of his country, in defence of her liberties, as long as he found his services useful to the state and the nation.

Having recovered Lorn he advanced Duncan to that heritage, which his brother's son had forfeited on account of his enlisting himself under the banner of Edward to fight against his country, and in these times of success acknowledged the brave Wallace as their Governor-General, and wise in the Cabinet and field. Noble Sir John Ramsay came to him with sixty fierce warriors, who had never been vanquished in the field at any former conflict with the English, in Strochane while he lay there and held Roxburgh, as the terror of the Saxon invaders.

Having thus settled Argyle, Lorn, Dunkeld, &c. he proceeded to reduce the Saxon garrison in Saint Johnston, where many brave Scots were confined as captives. The chieftain called Ramsay to him and disclosed his design on that fortress, saying, "In bonny St. Johnstown, which is situate on the banks of the river Tay, the Saxons rule with the arbitrary sway of lawful native lords. There I have set captives at liberty; there I have made the Saxons for Scotsmen die; but methinks I am not sufficiently avenged, till I kill ten thousand more, or expel them from our country. I wish to surprise its garrison, or battle down its proud walls, and level them with the ground." Ramsay, in council as wise, as brave in the field, answered, "that town cannot stand out long; the walls are low, the surrounding ditch narrow, although deep, our men will soon fill it, storm the place, and humble the pride of the garrison." Wallace was pleased with the decision, and the rode to Dunkeld, to prepare all their battering rams, and machines of war.

All things being ready, they carried them all down the river, with the best workmen they could hire, unto the devoted town. All their host assembled in St. Johnston, on the day that the machines arrived. In a very few hours the ditches were filled with earth and stones, in many places, and in others, floats of light timber were thrown across, the warriors quietly passed, raised batteries, and advanced to batter the walls.

Sir John Graham, Ruthven, and Sir John Ramsay beseiged the bridge, and Wallace surrounded the town. The Saxons made a desperate resistance.— They fought with new engines, casting large stones over the walls, upon the heads of the Scots. But Wallace forced his way, and passed over the walls with a thousand men. At the same moment, Sir John Graham and Ramham opened a breach and entered at the turret gate, and cut to pieces all who opposed them. Then a dreadful cry was raised in the town, and two thousand of the Southerons were put to the sword in the street. Sir John Stewart saw that the town was lost, and fled like a coward with sixty men in a barge towards Dundee, and left his host to die by the Scottish claymores.

Wallace remained four days in Saint Johnston, peopled it with Scots, and left Ruthven captain of the garrison, to keep the place. Then he marched off to reduce the Abbey of Cooper of Angus. The Abbot fled on his approach. So did the English in Glamis, Forfar, Breechin, Montrose, Mearns, &c. and collected themselves to the number of four thousand in Dunnoter Castle.

When Wallace arrived at Dunnoter, he offered them their lives, on condition they would leave the kingdom, but unfortunately they would not believe the sincerity of the Scots, and did not accept the overtures of merey; so he set fire to the church and burned them in it; the rest of them rushed out over the rocks, and fell headlong into the sea below. Not one remained alive! Wallace then marched on to

Aberdeen, seized all the goods and baggage of the Engligh in their ships, which were ready to sail burned the ships on the water. The enemy them selves burned the town but spared the priests, women and children, whom they always saved in their conquests.

After these dreadful exploits of retribution, he marched on to Buchan to surprise Beaumont, who, when he heard of the approach of Wallace fled to the Sloins, entered a ship, and returned to England. To Cromarty he winged his awful course, slew many of the Southerons, returned to Aberdeen, and proceeded to Dundee.

WALLACE LEAVES THE SIEGE OF THE CASTLE OF DUNDEE.

Defeats Cressingham at Stirling; causes the barons to swear allegiance to their king and country under his regency; appoints wise governors, skillful captains, sheriffs, &c. to govern the people in Bruce's absence and regulates the affairs of the nation.

Sir William Wallace, the Governor General, thought it prudent to raise the siege of the castle of Dundee, and march in all haste to Stirling to await the approach of Cressingham and Warren, who advanced with 60,000 men horse and foot, to re-conquer Scotland.

The traitor, Earl Patrick, joined the enemy at Tweed, and all marched to Stirling. Wallace received information of their coming, marched his men through St. Johnston, reviewed them in Sheriffmuir, and encouraged them in the language of a true patriot; so did Sir John Graham, in the ardour of his soul. "We have performed greater feats in the field, said he, with a smaller force, and made a stronger enemy yield, than the enemy that now comes to invade our country, murder our old men and children, deflour our virgins, pollute our wives and reduce us to chains and slavery." "Who fight, said Wallace, for just and righteous ends, God always sends them assistance. Then, though the enemy were ten thousand more, let us beat them as we have hitherto done, I purpose to contrive and set a snare for our enemies at Stirling bridge, and we will ensnare those fat loons to their destruction."

Wallace sends information every where to acquaint his friends that he would fight the Southerons on Tuesday at Stirling bridge. On Saturday he rode up to the bridge, place watches that no person might see or know what was going on with it. Then he ordered the good and skillful carpenter, John Wright to saw the boards which joined the bridge in two by the middle trest, to nail it on cornal bands, and to fill up the chasms with clay that nothing could appear He desired John Wright also to place the other end of the bridge on wooden rollers, in such a nice manner, that loosing one pin would precipitate the whole fabric in the gulf below. This being done he caused the carpenter to sit in a close cradle below the bridge, giving him strict orders to loosen the pin on the moment of time in which he should blow his horn.

The day of battle arrived, and the English advanced with all their force, full fifty thousand strong, six to one Scots warrior, yet the hearts of their chiefs knew no fear, and their men never shrunk. Ten thousand of the enemy surrounded the castle hill, thinking to possess fields and cattle at their will and pleasure; but the Scots kept close together on a plain field on the other side of the castle.

Then Hugh Cressingham led the vanguard on to battle with twenty thousand fierce warriors; Earl Warren with thirty thousand brought up the rear.—Cressingham passed the bridge with twenty thousand, and the Scots began to tnink it high time to blow the horn, but Wallace strode along the field leading on his men, till he saw Warren's host thicken on the bridge, when he snatched the horn from Jop, and blew both loud and shrill, and warned John Wright to strike out the pin. Down sunk the bridge, men and horses, in the watery abyss below! Oh! what a fearful cry ascended to salute the ears of their astonished companions on either bank of the Forth, which separated the English army at that awful juncture!

Wallace, with his nine thousand hardy Scots, made a furious attack on the 20,000 under Cressingham, who had passed over before the bridge was let down, and repelled them five acres breadth in foul disgrace: Ramsay, Lundie, Boyd, and Graham made dreadful havoc among the retreating English.

Wallace on foot, goes amongst the very thickest of his foes, with his huge claymore and orby shield, in search of Cressingham. He saw him, and sheared his bloody way among the throng. He swung his dreadful claymore, and notwithstanding the armour or coat of mail of his fierce adversary, felled him dead on the spot, and none could rescue him.

When the English saw their commander slain, and ten thousand of their companions lying dead on the field, they fled in great confusion in every direction, and seven thousand were driven into the Forth to rise no more.

When Warren's men saw the appaling fate of their companions, and the unbroken ranks of the dauntless Scots, they fled to Dunbar, without one stroke of the sword.

Then Wallace sent his cavalry in close pursuit of the enemy, and killed prodigious numbers of them, no less than 30,000 fell of the English on that fatal day; while very few of the Scots were killed, and none of note, except Andrew Murray, who was a true-hearted Scot.

Wallace, in order to secure the peace of the kingdom, and fortify them against foreign invasion, by uniting all parties and conciliating them to his regency, took an oath of all the Scottish barons, of allegiance to be faithful to their king and country, and to acknowledge her Warden in protecting the kingdom during Bruce's absence. Even Sir John Monteith, Lord of Arron, readily took the oath to stand faithful to Wallace in the cause of freedom. All those who would not comply, he punished severely; some he condemned and executed as traitors; some he imprisoned, and others he banished the kingdom, and his fame was heard throughout all the kingdoms of Europe.

After settling the affairs of the nation, Wallace returned and took the castle of Dundee by a stratagem and gave the English captains their liberty. So that in the course of ten days, no captain remained among them, except in the castle of Roxburgh and of Berwick, which Wallace intended to reduce, as soon as he could safely leave the cabinet to grace the field.

Chrystal Seaton, a Baron of grear fame who never deserted his country during their struggle for freedom posted himself with 40 men in Iedburgh wood, and harassed the English on all sides the fastness. And when he perceived that Heabottle, the English captain who commanded Iedburgh, fled from the castle with seven score of men, for fear of Wallace, he sallied forth from the wood, slew the captain and most of his men, took all their riches and stores, which they expected to carry with them to England. Seaton then placed Ruthven with a garrison in the castle, and marched into Lothian.

Scotland then enjoyed peace and traquillity for five months, under the regency of the brave Wallace.

A CONVENTION OF THE STATES CALLED,

To settle all the affairs of the kingdom, at St. Johnstown—Corspatrick refuses to acknowledge Wallace regent; mocks the summons to attend the Covnention; Wallace discomfits him in battle and expels him from the kingdom.

Corspatrick mocked the summons of the Lords of the Convention, and would not appear among them as one of them in the defence of Scotland under Wallace.

"We have great need,answeredCorspatrick to the call, now of a king, when Wallace reigns as governor. I am king of Kyle: I cannot understand how I should swear allegiance to him, I never held a furrow of land from him. I am as free to reign in this realm, Lord of my own lands, as any lord, prince or king; I also possess great lands in England, and no subject can demand fealty of me. I deride your call."

On reading Corspatrick's disdainful answer, Wallace could not be silent, and thus addressed the Lords of the Convention:

"My Lords, there can be none but one king who can, at once, reign over this realm. If Earl Patrick takes such ways and is thus allowed to insult the states, I plainly see that we are in a worse condition than we were in before; I am, therefore, of opinion, that he ought to be made to do homage to his lawful king." &c.

They all agreed that submission was absolutely necessary; and Wallace, the commander in chief of the forces, took his leave of them and marched away to Kinghorn with 200 men. He received additional troops under brave Seaton and Robert Lauder at Musselburgh and Lyle, with 20 men at Lintown, and marched past Dunbar in pursuit of Corspatrick.— The Earl marshalled nine hundred in the field of Innerwick, as Wallace advanced with four hundred strong, and furiously attacked Earl Patrick's host.– The conflict was long and bloody, but Earl Patrick was forced at last to retreat from the field of battle.

Wallace pursued him with three hundred men, by Cockburn , and passed on to the Bunkle-wood; but Corspatrick fled to Norham, and thence into England

Wallace then marched to the west to raise more troops, in order to prepare for the return of the English, whom he suspected to invade Scotland and be avenged on him.

Corspatrick and Bishop Beck, meantime, raised all the men of Northumberland, in compliance with the orders of King Edward, who also ordered Robert Bruce to proceed against Wallace and his country, having made him believe that Wallace had assumed his throne. Thus from Oyss to the Tweed passed an army of 30,000 men.

A squadron of ships were sent from the Thames to watch Dunbar and act in concert with their land forces. Corspatrick beseiged Dunbar which was then commanded by Chrystal Seaton. Wallace in good time returned with five thousand brave Scotsmen to rescue noble Seaton. He halted all that night at Yester, where Hay joined him with fifty good experienced horsemen, and counselled Wallace to give Corspatrick battle immediately.

Corpatrick and Beck ordered their men to lay in ambush near Spotsmuir, so that Wallace knew not of the stratagem. At last Wallace discovered Corspatrick marching furiously over a plain field with a very great host. The Scots thought themselves too few to engage 20,000 men, and deemed it prudent to retire to some place of strength, or to go and collect more warriors. Wallace said, "that would be a dangerous chance and expedient, while a furious enemy is rushing upon us. I will never flee as long as I have one against their four : there are twenty here this very day that would encounter them though I was absent ; if such be numerous, we are strong let us up and fight them ; they wont stand long."

A dreadful conflict ensued, and five thousand of the English fell at the first onset, and the rest were put in great confusion, but Earl Patrick encouraged and rallied his men to renew the combat ; but Wallace and Ramsay, Graham and Lundie, Seaton and Adam Wallace, Hay and Lyle, Boyd and Barclay, Baird and Lauder, pressed so furiously on them, that they were obliged to retire with great slaughter.

Just as the English began to flee, Bishop Beck caused his ten thousand men to sally from their ambush, and to attack and surround the Scots on every side.

When Wallace saw them so quickly appear, he deemed it expedient to retreat in close columns, but they were so completely surrounded, that they had to cut their way through them. The dreadful Patrick sought Wallace through all the throng, and wounded him even through his coat of mail. Wallace then mustered all his strength, and aimed a blow at him ; it missed him but clave Maitland down. Wallace was then completely surrounded by the English, and his horse being slain, was left alone on foot. Earl Patrick commanded his men to bear him down with spears, but like a champion brave, stood on his feet and hewed off their heads and scorned to yield.—Meantime the Scots missed Wallace and understood that he was alone or taken, and bold Graham, Lauder, Lyle, Hay, Ramsay, Lundie, Boyd, and Seaton, brought five hundred horsemen, rescued their beloved chieftain, and rode off to the main body. Two thousand more of the English fell in the second encounter; and the Scots, in all, lost only 500 men, and not one chief was slain in that battle.

After this glorious victory, all the country flocked to the standard of Wallace; Crawford of Edinburgh brought four hundred men, all in bright armour; Sir William Douglass also came with four score brave men, and others came from Tiviotdale and Jedburgh, and soon made up two thousand brave warriors, who immediately proposed to pursue their enemies, retreating on Lammermuir, in that same night and to be avenged on them. Wallace ordered his army to march in two divisions, three thousand under the command of Graham, Seaton, Lauder and Hay, and three thousand five hundred under his own, with Douglass, Ramsay, Barclay, Boyd, Lundie, and Adam Wallace, who at the rising of the sun, surprised the English, unprepared to fight, rushed upon them furiously with their broad claymores, and cut them to pieces.

Just as the English were engaged with Wallace under Beck, Sir John Graham led on his men from the ambush, and on his approach, ten thousand of them fled with Corspatrick and Beck and Bruce, to Norham house. The Scots pursued and made great havoc among them. 20,000 English perished that day by the sword!

Wallace, on his return to St. Johnston, passed over Corspatrick's lands, took away all his goods and demolished his castles, even to the number of twelve, within the Merse and Lothian. He then marched through Edinburgh and landed in Perth, and informed the barons of all his battles and successes, and received the thanks of the states, and dealt the rebels' lands to those who deserved them in fighting the battles of their country.

ALLACE MARCHES INTO ENGLAND,

Remains there nine months and returns without battle.

Wallace having established the affairs of the kingdom in a secure state, he entered England in the beginning of November, with an army of forty thousand Scots, all volunteers, on purpose to obtain provisions for them during the cold winter, because famine was endured, by a long and desolating invasion.

He began at the river Tweed to march his army, and spared neither man nor beast; burned all towns in Northumberland, even Durham was committed to the flames. Churches, abbeys, priories, convents, women and children were spared; corn and cattle became their lawful prey, in return for what they had done to Scotland.

All the inhabitants of Northumberland fled with their families and goods to New-Castle, on the approach of the Scots army, who ravaged the country between Tyne and Derwent, for the space of 20 days, and sent much spoil home to their famishing countrymen

Wallace then marched to Carlisle, and summoned the city to surrender; but, on refusal, he turned his attention to attack Berland, Allerdale and the country as far as Cockermouth, because he had no battering engines to beat down its proud walls. He next marched to New-Castle, and when passing the village of Kyton, the inhabitants confiding in the impossibility of Wallace reaching them, who were surrounded with water, insulted the Scots with opprobrious language as objects of derision, but Wallace and his men swam through the water, burned down their village, turned their laugh into mourning, and they fled with precipitation in every direction. He burned the towns of New-Castle and Durham, but the castles were left unreduced for want of battering rams.

Wallace next marched to York, slew all men in arms who opposed them, and burned the city, carrying off the spoils. Always as he passed, he levelled small forts and castles with the ground.

He spent fifteen days about the walls of York, and there Edward sent a knight to entreat him to cease from burning and slaying, promising that he would give him battle in fifteen days. Wallace answered, "I will desist both from fire and sword for forty days, if Edward will keep his promise and meet me on the field." Edward did set his hand and seal to this promise, and Wallace marched off the second day after, and pitched his tents in the northwest near Northallertown, and proclaimed peace for forty days. There Sir Ralph Raymont attempted to surprise Wallace and cut them to pieces. But some of his spies got information of the stratagem and revealed it to Wallace. He then called Richard Lundie and Hugh Hay, and commanded them to proceed in front with three thousand men, and there to lay in ambush in profound silence and secrecy and drew up his host in noble array. Raymont then advanced with seven thousand horsemen, but the Scots sallied forth from their ambush and attacked them furiously in the rear and laid three thousand of them dead at the first onset, with Ralph Raymont, their commander,and forced the rest to flee. Wallace pursued them to Milton, killed great numbers of them, and seized the town with all its riches and stores, regaled his men with English wine, ale, beef and bread, then burned the town, levelled its walls, and returned to his camp, which he then caused to be fortified, with a deep ditch around them.

Edward, then at Pumfret, sent to Wallace, promising to give him battle, on condition he would be crowned king of the Scots, and thereby become his equal, but Wallace could not be caught in that net. Sir A. Campbell and Earl Malcom and the rest, agreed that he should be crowned; but Wallace absolutely refused, saying, " it would be presumtuous; I would be a rogue to usurp the crown—I will fight for my king and my country, and God above will reward me in the end."

Woodstock counselled the nation, in Parliament, not to go out and meet Wallace, for they would be defeated; concluding, that the best method was to starve him out, by withholding all grain and cattle from his grasp.

Forty days being now expired, no English army appeared, and Wallace burned down North-allentown and proceeded to besiege York, spreading destruction through York wherever he went, saving women children and holy places.

SIEGE OF YORK.

Wallace commanded his eight captains, Lauder Malcom, Boyd, Campbell, Ramsay, Graham, Crawford, and Auchenleck, at the head of four divisions, two to each division, and the four divisions to attack the four gates of the city, with a thousand Scots archers for every gate. Seventeen thousand English then appeared on the walls, boldly using the bow and spear, furiously sallying out to repel them, but received a warm reception from the Scots, and were driven back within their walls. They then cast faggots of fire, red hot bars of iron, stones, burning pitch, and every prodigious thing, to gall the besiegers, who on the first day, only burned the bulwarks of the town, and cast the turrets down.

Next morning at break of day they encompassed the walls in the same manner, and galled the besieged severely with their arrows, set fire to every gate, but could not reduce the town that day, and they retired at night.

Meantime, in the dead of the night, the English, under the command of Sir Wm Morton and Sir Wm.

Lees, made a furious sally out with five thousand men, on Earl Malcom, in order to surprise them and cut them to peices.

Wallace, as he rode around watching the motions of the enemy, saw them coming and blew his martial horn, roused all his warriors, who lay in their harness, and led them to meet the enemy, with their claymores. Wallace rode briskly up and made a grand charge, and drove them again within their walls, leaving Sir John Morton dead upon the ground, with 1200 of his men to grace the field of battle.

Next day the Scots for the third time surrounded the town and assaulted the gates.—Just when their provisions were done, the English, not knowing the condition of the Scots, beat a parley. Wallace appeared and asked them what they meant by it.—The major in the name of the rest, promised to pay a ransom if the Scots would withdraw. Wallace replied, "we value not your gold—your king promised to give us battle ; let him act faithfully. The major answered very corteously, "He is the king, and we are but subjects ; take the gold and retire."

Wallace consulted with his captains and officers, who agreed to take the gold, because victuals were scarce, the place strong, themselves fatigued ; and to return to their native land, with booty. Wallace said, "I shall not be content, except they let the Scots banners wave upon the walls in sight of both armies, from eight in the morning till twelve at noon."

They received five thousand pounds of English gold, paid down in specie to their army that day, and plenty of provisions were conferred upon them for the twenty days they remained in York city after the capitulation.

As they marched homeward, they burned all Myldlame, levelling the towers, killing the deer in the forests, and breaking down parks and buildings.—Wallace then turned on the opulent Shire of Richmond ; burned Ramswatch and killed Fechew, the captain, and five hundred men.

Wallace then caused the widow of Fechew to carry her husband's head to London, and tell Edward, that Wallace had sworn by all the Fates, to be at London gates ; and that he would march with fire and sword through the south-west of England.

They spared the whole country of Saint Alban on account of the friendship of the Prior.

HE QUEEN OF ENGLAND PROCEEDS TO WALLACE WITH OVERTURES OF PEACE.

After the parliament of England concluded on making overtures of peace to conquering Wallace, no man could be found to be the embassy on such a commission ; but the Queen offered her services, and was commissioned to treat for peace.

As soon as Wallace saw the Queen with a glorious retinue of females and priests, and had finished the usual ceremony of receiving his illustrious guest, he asked her, "Madam, how do you like our encamping here?" The Queen answered, "Sir, very well ; but we need your friendship—God grant we may speed in this our errand."

Then Wallace withdrew and called a council of war, and warned them against the subtleties of woman and the dangers of treating with such a personage, in point of fidelity and confidence. After that they served up a handsome dinner and the Queen treated all the Scottish captains with every rich dainty.

Wallace, after the council had decided on their conduct in this affair, calmly asked her what she intended in her journey ? "Peace," answered the Queen, "we have no other thought, this raging war has wrought our destruction, grant it, Sir, for his sake that died for us." "Madam," said Wallace, "you ask no peace but for your own selfish ends, which can never compensate for the injustice done to our royal prince, in case of the arbitration between him and Baliol, his competitor, and for the other injuries done to the people in invading and laying waste the country." Hesilrig's cruelty, the hanging of our barons, the repeated violations of treaties, &c. at the rehearsal and remembrance of which Wallace and the Queen wept. "Wallace," she said, "we shall cease from this kind of discourse," and told three thousand pounds of English gold down, in his presence. Wallace then said "Madam, I will not grant you peace in the absence of your king ; with ladies, Madam, I cannot make a truce lest your false king break it ;" so the conference broke up and she returned to tell of the greatness of the Scot's hero and his brave army, and counselled parliament to send able men to treat with the chieftain of Scotland.

Lords Clifford, Beaumont, and Woodstock, came commissioned to treat with Wallace, and the last of these debated very subtly, but Wallace told him plainly that he used sophisms, and that they should restore Roxburgh and Berwick, their king Robert, Randell, Lord Lorn, Earl Buchan, Cumming, Soules, &c. so they concluded a peace for five years.

Thus Wallace delivered Scotland the first time from the English yoke, but they behaved so artfully that the nation should not see their king during the lifetime of Wallace.

WALLACE INVITED TO THE COURT OF FRANCE.

Leaves Lord James Stewart, Steward of Scotland, Governor in his absence.

Wallace, on the invitation of the king of France proceeded with fifty men to that kingdom. But they had not been more than two days at sea, before they saw sixteen sail of heavy ships bearing down upon them, having *red colours* flying, and the master of the vessel apprehended them to be pirates, under the personal command of Red Reaver, the tyrant of the seas, as they really happened to be the same monsters, who spared no lives for gold and other property, said the master; and their commander delights in blood and rapine.

Wallace encouraged him and enquired into the marks whereby he could distinguish him among his men. "At first sight you will ken him," said the master, "and will soon distinguish him from his men; a handsome proper man as there is in all France, and of a manly Scot's countenance, taller than any of his men a great deal, clothed with scarlet above a coat of mail, the foremost ship that pursues us, so he sails and you will quickly know it. He will enter first himself to enter our ship. There is a bar of blue in a shining shield, the badge of a christian, a band of white desiring aye the field, and the red betokens blood and hardihood."

Wallace ordered the shipmaster and seamen to go below, and then commanded his fifty men to lie close down upon deck, all clothed in bright armour, as an ambush to deceive the pirates, and ordered William Crawford, whom he placed at the haulyards to haul down the sails when he should hail them, and Cleland to lay the helm along the board at the same moment.

The Red Reaver came along side, and they received the salute "Strike dogs, or ye shall die," and they immediately hauled down the sails. The Red Reaver entered foremost and fearless, but Wallace grappled him by the gorget and threw him down upon deck, and his mouth and nose produced blood in abundance. The Red Reaver looked about with his visage pale; saw Wallace draw his dagger, and cried for mercy in the Latin language, and Wallace took all his weapons and spared his life, and caused him to swear on his word, that he should never fight against them or any other nation. that he should command all his men in the rest of his ships to cease from firing and war.

The Red Reaver then held up a glove, and all his men ceased immediately from firing, and Wallace took them all into Rochelle, during their voyage to Rochelle, the conversation turned on the way in which the Red Reaver first entered on a pirating life. "What countryman," said Wallace, "art thou?" "A Frenchman, Sir, and my father too;" answered Red Reaver. "How camest thou to this way of life?" "By mischance, Sir, it was from a great strife; at Court I killed a man, and was obliged to flee my country, I seized an English ship at Bordeaux, and set out a pirating, and thus I have lived on rapine and blood these sixteen years. I have conquered many, but in spite of fate, I am vanquished by one. Thus I confess to my eternal disgrace, my bloody life. "But pray, Sir," continued Red Reaver, "what is your name, that you, with your own single valiant hand, have commanded me all my sixteen sail; sure none except the Scots champion, brave Wallace, could thus have baffled me and all my fourteen hundred men. None whom I know should dare to encounter me, and I should esteem it a great honour to serve in his war." Then Wallace smiled, and answered modestly, "Scotland has need of many such as thee, what is thy real name?" said Wallace, Thomas of Loungeville," answered Red Reaver.—"Well deserve thy name, yea, our strife shall end here," answered Wallace, "if thou wilt repent and mend thy life, I will ever be thy faithful friend; I am that same Wallace whom thou dost now see." Then Loungeville fell down upon his knees, as if Wallace had been a crowned head, saying, "I am pleased much more that I have fallen into your hands, than that I had gotten sixty score of florins." Wallace concluded, "that since you have by chance fallen into my hands, and since the king has sent for me, I will tell him that I want your peace and pardon for my reward." Loungeville said, "if you could obtain my pardon, I would most faithfully serve thee all my days." But generous Wallace would take no advantage of his situation, and only desired mutual friendship.

Wallace proceeded to the king of France with Thomas of Loungeville, and obtained pardon for him and all his men, and the king even knighted him on the spot, and henceforth he went and fought with Wallace in all his succeeding wars in Guienne and in Scotland.

WALLACE ARRIVES AT THE FRENCH COURT, AND CONQUERS GUIENNE.

Philip, king of France, received Wallace most courteously, and honourably, and all his nobles vied with each other in marks of respect to the Scots hero. Wallace then requested permission to make war upon the English at Guienne, and he in several great battles conquered them, and drove them ou of that territory, and restored it to its original propri etors, but the king to reward his services, made him Lord of all Guienne, as John Blair writes.

When the English parliament heard of Wallace's fighting for Philip of France, they pretended that he had broken the peace, and that they would again invade Scotland by sea and by land, and reduce it to a Roman province. So they sent a great army of foot and horse, and a fleet of many sail, who in conjunction took Bothwell Castle, Saint Johnston, Dundee, and all the country from Cheviot to the sea, plundering and murdering men, women and children, and all the old friends of Wallace, who governed the realm in his absence, were forced to flee and hide themselves; so the sanguinary Edward made a second conquest of Scotland.

Adam Wallace, Robert Boyd, Lundie, John Graham, and Hugh Hay, however, with about fifty men, soon commenced a defensive war, by intercepting their provisions, and cutting of straggling parties. they first surprised four score of the guard of provisions coming to Bothwell Castle, and killed sixty of them, and took all their gold and goods, while five Scots only fell in the engagement. Meantime Guthrie sent to Wallace, and intreated him to come home, and fight again for their laws and liberties.

Wallace soon appeared again on the field, in defence of their injured rights, and in vengeance of the slaughtered sons of his native Caledonia. For he landed at Montrose with his brave companions, and Longueville, and was joined by Sir John Ramsay, Ruthven, Bissett, Barclay, and others, making a martial company of three hundred men, whom he marched to Ochter house, determined to liberate his country or die in the cause of freedom.

WALLACE RE-TAKES ST. JOHNSTON BY STRATAGEM.

With his small band, Wallace marched speedily to Perth, a place of great importance, in the heart of the kingdom, admitting of communication from England by sea. As he lay in ambush in the vicinity watching an opportunity to surprise the English, it fortunately happened that six English servants came forth with empty carts, to convey hay into the town. Wallace instantly slew the servants, and arrayed themselves with the upper garments, loaded the carts with hay, and as many as could, secreted themselves in the loads of hay, and six drove the carts, the rest lay in ambush very near, to seize every opportunity that might be given them to enter the town. In this disguise they entered the town, and Wallace slew the sentinel or porter, and secured the gates for the entrance of his brave men, who immediately appeared and spread destruction in every quarter among the surprised English, which so terrified the rest, that Sir John Stewart, the governor, fled out at the gate to Methun wood, a hundred took refuge in the church, but the superstition of Wallace did not induce him on such an occasion to spare their lives, even in the sacred sanctuary. By this success Wallace acquired much booty, and a place of great importance in point of future conquests.

WALLACE MARCHES INTO FIFE,

Conquers the English at Blackironside, reduces Lockleven and Ayrth, and delivers the most part of the country.

Wallace then marches into Fife, and was attacked by Sir John Stewart from the Ochile-hills. The Scots being few in number were greatly alarmed at this sudden surprise and deemed it best to flee and get across the Tay, to receive assistance from their brave companions, who knew nothing of their danger. But Wallace saw they were all dead men if they attempted to flee, so he counselled them to be posted in the wood of Blackironside, and to raise a strong barrier of trees to keep them from being overpowered and borne down by numbers.

Stewart and Vallance, with their numerous host, attacked them, and surrounded the wood at the same time with great bravado, thinking to kill the one hundred Scots rebels without any trouble. Wallace thus addressed his men "take courage lads, and bravely show your face, the wood we will hold as long as we can stand, to the last man we will fight for it sword in hand, the right is ours, let us up to it manfully, I will free this land once more before I die," which did so engage their hearts to him, and raised their spirits that many were for rushing upon the enemy in the open plain, but Wallace wisely restrained their ardour. Wallace's forty good archers galled the English horse on every side in a most effectual manner; and the rest were spearmen who desired nothing but honour and glory in war defended their posts with valour and undauntedness, leaving a space for the English to enter; in order to get an advantage of them entering in at a narrow pass. The whole body of English made a second grand attack with the resolution to conquer and kill every one of the Scots, but they were again repulsed with great slaughter, 180 of them laid dead on the field, then Stewart caused his men to sound a retreat and consulted what was next to be done. He charged Vallance to watch all night, and keep Wallace into Cooper; but Vallance would not fight all day and watch all night, so a dispute arose between the two English commanders. Wallace took the advantage of this dispute and called on Vallance to come over to them and promised him a Lordship in the land. Vallance chose rather to take his chance with the Scots, than to venture his life in the hands of the enraged Stewart and Edward, so he came over with two hundred men. By this time, too, brave Ramsay and Ruthven came with three hundred men to Blackironside, and the whole band of Scots consisted of five hundred and sixty men, while Stewart drew up two thousand men on the plain; the Scots advanced boldly and attacked them, defeated and killed all but a few fugitives on the field of battle. Wallace himself cut Stewart down with his great claymore. Then Ruthven marches to Perth and takes it; Sir John Ramsay took Cooper of Fife ; Wallace and Crawford, Guthrie, Loungeville, and Richard took Lindores without any opposition, all the English having fled before them.

One company of English still remained in Lochleven, and Wallace could not rest, until he reduced it also ; so he marched off in the middle of the night with eighteen chosen men, whom he ordered to remain on the Loch, while he, himself, would swim with his sword to the castle and bring away their boat to carry them over.

They having obtained the boat, soon reached the Castle and boldly attacked it with sword in hand, and spared none, excepting women and children. They remained eight days there and received Ramsay with all his men, when they repaired to Perth where good Bishop Sinclair met him and counselled him to proceed with all alacrity : and Jop was sent to the north for supplies, and John Blair to the west in Priest's garments to warn their friends in the west ; and the people flocked to the standard of Wallace from every quarter of the land. Wallace then proceeded with fifty men and took Ayrth by surprise, killed Thomas Weir, the captain, and one hundred men, even all that were in the garrison, and delivered his uncle from chains. Before morning they had all the spoils conveyed away to Torwood, in the neighborhood, and marched off to Dumbarton.

Wallace and his men arrived at Dumbarton before break of day. He called upon a widow of his acquaintance who entertained them in a close barn with the greatest secrecy. She presented her nine sons to Wallace to increase the number of his warriors, and made him a present of one hundred pounds. Meantime he caused her to mark all the doors where the Southerons lodged and then marched all his men in solemn silence unto the gate where they securely slept. An English captain and nine of his messmates were still drinking and vaunting about their strength, one said, "Had I Wallace, I would think nothing to engage with him;" another said, "I would tie Sir John Graham," a third said "I will fight Boyd" and so on, and Wallace walks in among the midst of them and saluted them handsomely all round, "I am come from my travels, gentles," said he, "I long to see your conquest of the Scots, some of your good cheer I would wish to have." Then the Captain gave him a very saucy answer, saying, "Thou seemest to be a Scot, likely to be a spy, and mayest be one of Wallace's company, which, if thou be, nothing shall protect thee from being hanged. Wallace thought it then good time to draw his dreadful claymore, and he cut off his head at one stroke, killed another, and burned a third into the fire, and Kierly and Stephen came in and killed all the rest. And then by the guidance of a hostler, he set fire to the buildings where the rest of the English slept, and burned them all to death, and proceeded to reduce Roseneath Castle.

The night following the fall of Dumbarton, Wallace proceeded from Dumbarton Cave, whither he retired for rest, after the burning the English there, to Roseneath where he surprised and killed eighty of them returning from a wedding, entered the castle along with the fugitives, and slew all the garrison, and having feasted a few days on the spoils, burned and abandoned it. He then marched to Falkland to meet Earl Malcom, Richard Lundie, Sir John Graham, Adam Wallace, Barclay, Boyd, &c. and to keep his yool and holy days. Then he heard of the decease of his good old mother, and despatched Jop and Mr. Blair to bury her decently, and proceeded to the liberation of his country from a foreign yoke.

SIR WILLIAM DOUGLAS WINS THE CASTLE OF SANQUHAR BY A STRATAGEM,

And rescued by Wallace from falling into the hands of their cruel enemies.

Although Sir William Douglass was constrained to submit to the English, and to marry an English lady, he took the castle of Sanquhar by stratagem, put every man to the sword, inclosed himself in the castle, and sent a messenger to entreat Wallace to bring him speedy relief. Meantime Wallace began to march south, and, in his route, cut off Ravendale, an English captain, with two hundred men, in the vicinity of the Castle of Kilsyth; in the same route he burned the towns of Linlithgow, Dalkeith and New-Castle, expelling the English from every place of strength. He proceeded then to Peebles, where he received reinforcements of one hundred men under Lauder and Seaton, who has just issued from the Bass, and forty or fifty more with Hugh Hay, and sixty with Rutherford, making an army of eight hundred strong. By this time the English had beseiged sir William Douglas in Sanquhar, and just as he was about to proceed on his conquering march, Dickson, Douglas' messenger, arrived, and requested speedy assistance of Wallace. Without a moment's delay, Wallace marched to his aid. The English who besieged the castle flew when they heard the approach of William Wallace, with the greatest precipitation. Wallace being informed of their flight, pursued them with three hundred horsemen, overtook and routed them at Closeburn with great slaughter.

During the pursuit their horses failed, but the men like lions and hinds, pursued them on foot, till the English diappeared ; even five hundred dead bodies were strewed through the fields. Wallace immediately after these successes, received continual fresh troops, horses and men. Currie, Johnston, Kirkpatrick and Halliday, with seven score of new men, joined him at Closeburn. Then he rode to Dumfries, and proclaimed peace to all who would assist against the Southerons, for the English had almost all left the kingdom, and the places of strength were again occupied by Scotsmen.

While Wallace was besieging Dundee, the last place he had to reduce, Edward being convinced of the impossibility of conquering Wallace and the Scots by dint of arms, plotted how he might ensnare him by bribes, promises or honours, which gained the submission of others, &c. All his pretences, &c. were in vain Wallace answered Edward's emissaries in the following words, "I owe my life to, and will willingly lay it down for my country, although all other Scotsmen should submit to the king, I never will give obedience or yield allegiance to any power, except to the king of Scotland, my rightful sovereign."

King Edward finding no stratagem could succeed to draw Wallace into the snare, he sent Lord Woodstock with ten thousand men to march to Stirling bridge, to secure that pass, until he should come up with the main body, but Wallace heard of Woodstock's coming, and drew up his eight thousand on Sheriffmuir, where the two armies joined battle, and the Scots fought most furiously, and cut ten thousand English down on the spot, for they would not flee, not one of them escaped the claymore that day, and all their horses, silver, gold, arms and other spoils, were a rich booty to the surviving Scots, who then retired beyond the bridge and broke down all the passes, and proceeded to secure Dridfoord against the enemy. Wallace then received more reinforcements with Earl Malcom, Sir John Graham, Stewart, of Bute, Cummings, of Badanoch, making an army of 30,000 strong, who marched to Falkirk, to meet Edward's host of one hundred thousand warriors. But, alas, Cumming instigated Stewart to dispute the right of being commander in chief with Wallace, claiming the right to lead the vanguard, and fled with his ten thousand, and Wallace withdrew his ten thousand, and left Stewart to encounter the whole English army, who cut them all to pieces, but not without the tremendous loss of thirty thousand killed on the field of battle.

By this time Wallace was surrounded, and was compelled to cut his way through Bruce's host, and there the Scots again stretched eight thousand Southerons on the field as they cut their way through them, and proceeded to the Torwood. Wallace, Graham and Lauder remained behind the army with three hundred men, and attacked the enemy's wing, and there killed three hundred more; but they were at tacked by thirty thousand under Bruce, and were so entangled in rescuing each other, and fighting their retreat, that they lost Sir John Graham, and were forced to swim across Carron river, leaving in all, ten thousand more of their enemies dead on the field. Next day he proceeded to the field, discovered the body of Graham, and entombed him under the following Epitaph:

"*Mente Monuque potens et Vallac fidus Achates*
Conditur hic Gramius bello,inter fectus abAnglis."

Wallace proceeded then to Linlithgow, and surprised the English in their tents, killed ten thousand of them, and the rest fled, losing three thousand in the flight ; but the Scots pursued them out of the land, and then returned to Edinburgh. Thus Wal lace delivered Scotland a second time from the Eng lish yoke.

WALLACE MEETS THE PARLIAMENT,

And resigns his commission and returns to France, conquered John Lynn at sea and the country of Guienne.

On account of some jealousies Wallace resigned the command of the Army, and the office of Governor General of Scotland, and retired to France, where he received great honours and praise. He embarked with eighteen of his brave followers at Dundee, and as they steered along the English coast about the Humber, they saw a sail bearing down upon them. They soon discovered with fear that it was John Lynn, the cruel and bloody pirate of the seas. Wallace sent all the trembling cowards below, and steered the ship himself. John of Lynn with seven score of rogues came along side, galled the Scots with guns before they clasped, but when they clasped the Scottish spears made dreadful havoc among them for nearly an hour ; the merchants too in their woollen harness, behaved themselves like gallant men in that fight, killed or drowned all the seven hundred men and took their gold &c. The King knighted Wallace as soon as he arrived in France, and gave him gold to support the war in Guienne against the English, where he marched with 10,000 men, and laid waste all Guienne, conquered it in five pitched battles, and was made Lord of that land.

WALLACE SURPRISED, BUT CONQUERS THE TRAITORS

After he had made a conquest of Guienne, he iv ed like a prince at Shemon, until a proud knight of France boldly claimed sundry lands and an office in Guienne as his hereditary right which were then in Wallace's hands, and contrived a hellish plot to cut him off, and then to obtain re-possession of his lands. Pretending good services to Wallace, he made an ap pointment to meet him with fifteen men each at a certain place. The treacherous knight, knowing the strength and valour of the Scots and his own deep design, brought forty armed men and placed them in ambush, to sally forth as soon as the dispute should begin in order to destroy him. Then the knight arrived and began to speak in an angry tone, saying, " Thou dost possess my lands by no good right."— " I have no lands," Wallace replied, " but what the king gave me, and what I have won in peril of my life from the English in a bloody contest." " Then," answered the knight sternly, " thou shalt here resign them or die, by the powers divine," and drew his sword and the whole ambush rushed out and surprised the Scots. " Are these the thanks," said brave Wal lace, " I receive from your hands, for restoring of your native lands ? Although I and these my men want armour, sixteen against your fifty-five, what then ? Here's a claymore made of the truest steel, which thy deserving neck shall shortly feel," and with one single stroke cut down the treacherous knight and bid him to purchase a grave for himself. Then the fifty-five Gallic warriors surrounded Wallace and his fifteen men, who like brave Scots, with noble hearts and true, fought boldly and cut down heaps of Frenchmen.—The knight's brother fought long and bravely, but they were all cut down at last. In sight of this bloody contest nine Frenchmen were mowing hay, who, when they saw their countrymen worsted and stretched on the plain advanced with all speed, each armed with a sharp scythe, and made a dreadful attack, as if nothing could impede their fury. Wallace, as soon as he descried the scythe men coming, immediately advanced in head of his men towards the clowns.—The first of them made a dreadful cut at Wallace, but he being strong, tight and swift, overleaped his scythe, and cut his head from his shoulders with a back stroke of his claymore. He jumped over the next fellow's scythe, and clave his shoulder more than half a yard. He leaped over the third's scythe, and killed him also, and the fourth he clave through the body, and the fifth he pursued and slew also. So having despatched five and put the other four to flight, he returned to his brave men who had, by that time, slain forty-nine of the Frenchmen—and seven fled off the field of battle.

The King of France was exceedingly glad at the success and victory of Wallace over such a treacherous murderer, and invited him earnestly to remain at court as one of his own household, and live happy and secure under his royal protection. Wallace ac cepted the offer, and remained two years at the French court, being diverted with princely sports, in favour with kings, lords, and ladies.

WALLACE INSULTED BY TWO CHAMPIONS,

Fights and kills them both.

While Wallace lived at the French court, two Gallic Champions, who mortally hated the Scots, always passing their satirical jokes on Scotsmen and Scotland, so enraged our brave champion, that he could no longer endure such insults. These two champions used always to walk linked in each others arms, and it happened one day that Wallace was in a large hall, where none did wear arms, and was grossly insulted by them, and he asked them, " What means all this hatred, when our nations live in firm alliance and friendship ? Did we deserve good words for our good deeds ? What would you say of your proud enemies, when you talk so of your friends ? They disdainfully replied in their own language, " The English are our foes, we own, but the Scots for falsehood are known every where ;" at which Wallace was so enraged, that he gave one of them a foundering blow and made his nose bleed profusely ; the other tnen struck at Wallace, supposing his compan ion dead on the floor, but Wallace clasped him so hard, that his soul departed from his body; the other had recovered by this time, and again encountered him with fury, but Wallace dashed out his brains upon a pillar, saying " Let them take that for their pains —what the devil ailed the carles, they were to blame; it would have been long before I would ever have troubled them. Let all young persons learn from this example how to bridle their tongues." Many of the great lords of France were displeased at this unfortunate conflict, became jealous, and hated Wallace; but the king exonerated him from all blame on this occation, and none durst cast a saucy look at him.

WALLACE AND THE KING DECEIVED BY THE LORDS, WAS LED TO FIGHT THE LION.

As the king loaded Wallace with marks of respect and honour, his nobles became envious, hateful and malicious towards him, and two of them plotted hellishly, to effect the destruction of the brave Scots hero, to be avenged on him for the death of the two champions, their near relations, and to sacrifice the life of the Scot in an ignominious manner. These two squires come to the king, forged a lie, saying, " this Scot brags and boasts, and says, that he would undertake to fight your lion, if you will freely give him your permission, and he has desired us to ask your leave, we are sure he will have a difficult task." The King replied with great concern, "I am sorry he desireth such a thing, yet I will not deny whatever favour he may ask me while he is in France." They then went to Wallace, fabricated another story, saying, 'Wallace, the king commands you fight his lion without further commands.' Wallace replied, 'whatever is the will of the king, I will most gladly fulfil with all my strength," then instantly repaired to court. A lord at court, when he saw Wallace there, most foolishly asked him, if he durst fight the fierce lion? he answered. yes, truly, if the king would have me to do so, or with yourself, I fear none of the two, let cowards from kings courts be all debarred, I may be worsted, but never shall be dared, so long as my nostrils retain the breath of life or Scottish blood circle in my veins, like a true Scot I will fight and scorn to flee; for why, I know that man is made to die." Then the king granted that Wallace might fight the lion, without knowing the conspiracy laid against the life of the Scot, and brought harness for Wallace, but he said, no, I leave that to the field, Almighty God only shall shield me, since this is but a beast and not a man, with what I have I will fight as I can, and will encounter him single as I go, though this foe is a fierce, strong, rapacious, cruel and relentless enemy. Then he wrapped his mantle round one hand and took his claymore in the other, and proceeded to the place where the lion raged in expectation of blood. Wallace then thrust his covered arm into the lion's mouth, drew a stroke from neck to heel and cut him through the body, and then called aloud to the king, "Pray, Sire, is this your whole desire thus to expose me to the rage and will of your fierce lion; have you any more to kill? Cause them to bring them forth; such beasts I will quell and will obey you so long as I dwell in France. But now I take leave forever of France, some greater action I may soon achieve. At Shemon, sir, I thought the other year that you would have had other business for me here, than to fight a cruel savage beast, therefore I shall return to ancient Scotland once more." The king perceiving Wallace in anger, meekly replied, "It was your own desire, else by the faith of a most Christian king, I never would have allowed any such a thing, for men of honour asked it in your name, so you or they are only to blame." Wallace replied, "I vow to the great God, this seems to me a thing most strange; by all that is good, I know no more of it than a child unborn, this is a trick devised by some of those who are my secret and malicious enemies."—The king called the two squires and caused both their heads to be cut off on the judgment of their own confession.—Wallace perceiving himself to be envied by the French lords and having received a letter from the Scottish Barons entreating him to return, so he took his leave of the king and court, and proceeded, loaded with gold and jewels, to Scotland to fight for the rights and liberties of his native country. All the lords and ladies about the court grieved and wept on the departure of the Scots champion, hero, and knight; but no Scotsmen of note returned with him, only Longueville, who would never leave him.

WALLACE ARRIVES AT THE MOUTH OF ERNE,

In the river Tay, fights the battle of Elcho Park.

Wallace having arrived at the mouth of the Erne, he marched quietly with eighteen valiant men, to Elcho-Park: on his way he called at Crawford's house, his cousin's, who embraced and kissed him with joy and gladness of heart, and secured his men till they were rested, refreshing them with food and drink, until Crawford proceeded to Perth to buy provisions, when the English noticed his buying of more provisions than usual, and seized him and laid him in prison; but after questioning him, let him go, and then armed eight hundred men, and dogged Crawford home. Crawford arrived and warned Wallace to flee, "for I greatly fear says he the rogues are at my heels; I will give you all the assistance I can give, I myself shall be the twentieth man." No sooner had the Scots issued forth in armour, than eight hundred English came in sight, and Butler at their head.—

When Wallace saw their numbers, he withdrew to Elcho Wood, and there fortified a pass with long trees across the path where they could enter, and on either side the place was naturally fortified by a close thicket of hollens, that defended them in the flanks and rear. Then he addressed his men as follows: "The wood is thick, its breadth and length is small, if we had food enough, we could keep the strength, meantime let us bravely fight as long as we can stand, for our old native country; come, let us to it, either do or die; ere they gain the pass, we shall lay some of their bellies to the wind." By this time Butler had Crawford's house surrounded, seized his wife, and vowed to burn her to death, if she did not tell where the Scots warriors had gone. Wallace having issued from the thicket to reconnoitre his enemies, and see the fate of his cousin's family, just when they were about to burn Mrs. Crawford, called aloud to them to "stay their hand, for here am I, and own myself your foe; why should ye torment an honest, innocent woman? come forth to me and we will end the strife; it were a prodigious sin to kill the female Scot, art thou a christian? tell me yea or nay; in all my victories, I always saved the priests, women and children." Butler threw his face, bit his lip, and heaved with venom and spite, when he saw brave Wallace in his presence.

Then the English fiercely marched after him, as he retired to his place of strength in the thicket, and attacked the Scots boldly at the pass, which was nobly defended, and were repulsed with the loss of fifteen men killed on the first onset. They made a second and more desperate attack in three divisions.

at three different points at the same moment. Wallace saw their divisions advance, and ordered his Longueville with six men, Crawford with six, to keep the weakest parts of the strength, and Wallace kept five with himself to meet Butler at the pass.—Wallace then allowed some men to come in, on purpose to ensnare them. Seven men entered, looked very timid, and were immediately cut down; but Butler withdrew from the entrance when he saw the fate of his men, and Longueville and Crawford made so grand a defence, that the enemy were forced to retire for the night.

Butler set his watches, and retired to feast on good provisions, while the wearied Scots had only water to drink; but Wallace, with cheerful countenance, and encouraging words, made a single night of fasting easy to them, and before morning, under the cover of a thick fog, sallied out upon the English, killed Butler and thirty of his men, carried wounded Crawford off the field, retired to Methven wood, marched off to Birnam wood, and thence to Athol and Lorn, where they were reduced to the last extremity by famine.

There, as Wallace slept alone in the woods, (for he had retired from his men, and had fallen asleep,) five sanguinary assassins, who had been bound, on pain of death, to take Wallace, dead or alive, drew near and attempted to bind Wallace; but he rose like a lion in his full strength, dashed the brains out of the first against a tree, despatched the other three with the dead man's sword, and two fled. The enraged champion pursued and smote them both to the ground. Wallace having found a boy with some provisions on the hill, and having fed his men with them, he marched directly to Rannoch plains where he found the castle commanded by Scotsmen, who received him into the fort, and promised to obey his commands, and swore allegiance to Robert Bruce under Wallace. The lord of the castle sent his three valiant sons, and twenty other brave warriors to fight the battles of their country, under the renowned chieftain of Scotland, who there displayed the Scottish banner, and marched through the country to recruit his army. He landed at Dunkeld, put all the garrison to the sword, feasted five days on good provisions, took all their gold and jewels, and returned again to the north, considering themselves too few to besiege the town of Perth.

In Ross, Bute, Argyle, Buchan, Murray, &c. he collected an army of seven thousand men, and marched straight to Aberdeen. The English all fled on the approach of the invincible Wallace. Clement, the brave knight of Ross, came to Wallace with a gallant company of warriors ; Sir John Ramsay, also joined him, with many others, and he then deemed his power sufficient to place and keep judges over the land, and establish garrisons in all strong holds.

SIEGE OF PERTH

Wallace having thus settled the government of the kingdom, proceeded immediately to reduce the castles remaining in the hands of the English. He first besieged Perth, and took it by storm, killing 1080 in the breach of, and round the walls, and garrisoned it by Scotsmen. Sinclair, Lundie, Lindsay, Boyd, Adam Wallace, Seaton, Lauder, Dundas, Scott, &c. fought with Wallace in that engagement.

Wallace then proceeds to the south, where he found that Edward Bruce had arrived from Ireland with fifty men of his mother's relations, and had already taken Kirkcudbright with a garrison of nine score: Wigtown castle he had also reduced, and joined Wallace most cheerfully, and then marched with him to Lochmaben, where Wallace like a true and faithful Scot, resigned the command of the army to him, promising to crown him king of Scotland, if his brother Robert did not come home to possess his throne.

Prince Edward Bruce remained in Lochmaben, but Wallace proceeded to Cummock ; so Scotland was the third time delivered by the brave and faithful Wallace, and then had rest from wars and ravages of their enemies.

MONTEITH BETRAYS WALLACE.

When king Edward found it impracticable to conquer and subjugate Scotland as long as Wallace lived, he called Aymer de Vallance to him, and consulted with him how he might betray him by his own friends. Edward promised to give him any thing he should ask, except his queen and crown, if he would take Wallace dead or alive. Vallance then proceeded to Bothwell to execute the hellish plot. He promise in Edward's name, to give John Montieth the Earldom of Lennox and three thousand pounds of English gold. "Fy," said Monteith, "it would be a mighty shame, yea, you and I would be very blameable, if we betrayed a man who had done so great services to his king and country; he is of our nation too, and is the governor of the land, and captain general of our forces; for my part I declare, come weel, come woe, I never will condescend to treat him so." Vallance replied, "if you did understand what a shedder of Christian blood he is, you would not plead for him, but rather contribute to break his power; besides the king has no desire to take away his lif, but to confine him so that both nations might ease from war, and that he should not disturb the c mo peace."

The poor souled Monteith began tnen to aver when he heard that he was not to be massacred, an having formerly wished him in Edward's power provided he would spare his life, he half resolved to take the bribe. Vallance when he saw Monteith thrown into hesitation, employed all his deep cunning and satanic art to induce him to accept of the bribe, and told him down three thousand pounds of English gold, saying "this you shall have and Lennox at your will, if you will now fulfil the king's desire."— Monteith could no longer resist the temptation, he received the gold and bound himself to carry Wallace and put him securely into the hands of the English ! ! !

Vallance merrily scampered off to London and left Montieth to fulfil his horrid contract ! Edward sent private letters to Monteith, urging him to execute quickly what he had undertaken. Monteith read over the letter and then called his sister's son, and caused him to swear to conceal the plot : "go" said Monteith, "and wait on Wallace as a domestic, and when a fit opportunity occurs, be sure to embrace it, and call me and I will secure him." The villain promised to fulfil all his commands.

Meantime, as the God of Providence would have it, Wallace wrote to Robert Bruce to come into Scotland and receive quiet possession of his throne and kingdom. Bruce returned a letter promising to meet Wallace on Glasgow muir on the first of July. So Wallace proceeded to Glasgow muir, and none understood where he went but Kierly, and the young traitor in Wallace's service, who on the eighteenth night warned Monteith, who caused sixty men to march from Dumbarton and to lurk near Glasgow town, and sent out a spy to notice the house where

Wallace resided. Rarbreston, or the cottage of Lumloch was its name, and as Wallace and Kierly went to sleep, the young fellow went out and informed his uncle of the fit time to secure him. Then Monteith called his sworn traitors to surround the house, slew Kierly and seized upon Wallace, who rose like a lion; but ah! his claymore, his dagger, and all were previously stolen away by his treacherous servant, and he could find nothing to use in his own defence except a bench by which he killed two of the traitors. At last Monteith spoke subtily to Wallace, and told him that the English surrounded the house, and that it would be in vain to make any resistance, a single man unarmed against a host of armed men under Clifford. They will save your life, so make no resistance, but come along to Dumbarton with me, and you will be as safe as at home; we have come to save your life, see we have no weapon; and Wallace believing all he said in the house submitted to their will, on condition that Monteith would fulfil his promise to save his life. "Only as a prisoner the English must see you" said Monteith "bound with cords, else they will take you from me." So they cunningly slipped cords on his hands, and bound them down with counter cords underneath, and led him bound to Solwaysands, and there delivered him into Vallance's and Clifford's hands, who first confined him in Carlisle prison, and afterwards conveyed him to the Tower of London. As he passed through England, great multitudes of men, women and children, assembled from all quarters of the land, to gaze upon the illustrious prisoner.

During his imprisonment there he occupied his few remaining days in holy devotion, especially delighting in his Psalter; and before his execution made his bequest to Helen Mar, his second wife, and bequeathed his private property to the brave Lanerkers, who first fought for their country, in the following words: "As the first who stemmed with me the torrent, which with God's help we so often laid into a calm, I mention to you my faithful Lanerkers. Many of them bled and died in the conquest; and to their orphans, with the children of those who yet survive, I consign all the world's wealth that yet belongs to William Wallace; Ellerslie and its estates are theirs. To Bruce, my sovereign and my friend, the loving companion of the hour in which I freed you, my Helen, from the arms of violence! to him I bequeath this heart, knit to him by bands more dear even than loyalty. Bear it to him; and when he is summoned to his Heavenly throne, then let his heart and mine fill up one urn. To Lord Ruthven, to Bothwell, to Scrymgeour, and Kirkpatrick, I give my prayers and blessings."

He was then conducted to the house of William Delect in Fen church-street, and the day following the 23d of August 1305, was brought to Westminster on horseback, accompanied with knights, the mayor, sheriff, and aldermen, and was placed on the south bench of the great Hall, crowned there in derision with a laurel, while Sir Peter Malory, the Chief Justice, impeached him with treason; to which he boldly replied: "I never was a traitor, nor could I be to the king of England." He impeached him also with burning towns, levelling castles, killing the English, &c. but Wallace considered these things all right in case of national war. But innocence became guilt at the bar of envy and malice, and all his heroic virtues were declared capital crimes, and he was tried by the laws, and hanged, drawn and quartered by the administrators of injustice in England.

His head was fixed on London bridge, and the four quarters of his body were placed on the gates of the four principal cities of his native country!

These acts of betraying, condemning, and butchering the greatest statesman, the best general, the most intrepid soldier, the most feeling benefactor of mankind that ever graced the annals of the world, incensed the Scottish nation beyond all bounds.

The brave, the generous, the disinterested William Wallace, the deliverer of his country, was thus betrayed and butchered. This was the greatest misfortune that could ever have befallen Scotland; it was inexpressibly afflicting to his friends and honest defenders; and who could have been so base as not to befriend the restorer of their liberties? even every peasant in the country, every shepherd on the hill, commisserated the fate of Wallace, and their hearts burned with a desire of avenging his blood on the head of Edward

As for Monteith, all men, his friends and enemies, considered him the basest of the human race, whose criminality will adhere to his name and family as long as Scotland is a nation. He became a traitor to his best friend! a traitor to his country! a betrayer of innocent blood! an assassin in heart and practice! and the ignominy of his treachery will be reflected on his happy posterity, while the annals of Scottish history record his deed! Hence the poet expresses the feelings of the nation upon the sad event of his death:

"Envious death, which ruins all,
Hath wrought this sad lamented fall
Of Wallace; and no more remains
Of him, than what an urn contains;
We ashes for our Hero have,
He for his armour a cold grave;
He left the earth, too low a state,
And by his acts o'ercome his fate;
His soul death had not power to kill;
His noble deeds the world do fill
With lasting trophies of his name.
O! hadst thou virtue lov'd or fame
Thou couldst not have exulted so,
Over a brave, betray'd—just foe,
Edward! nor seen those limbs expos'd
To public shame—fit to be clos'd
As relics, in a holy shrine,
But now the infamy is thine:
His end crowns him with glorious bays,
And stains the brightest of thy praise.
O false Monteith! your honour's gone,
Your fame is lost, the deed is done!
A traitor to your country's son,
The bravest e'er her laurels won.
You did him cast in London Tower,
In Edward's hands' and Edward's power;
Innocent blood you offer'd free,
A sacrifice for Liberty.

You the price of blood received,
The bravest of the brave deceived;
Now infamy will haunt your name,
As traitor's everlasting shame.

Few princes have had the honour of such an illustrious captain, or such an opportunity to immortalize their fame, by an act of generous magnanimity, either to treat him with kind hospitality, or to liberate him with princely greatness. Few Princes could have been so base, mean and sanguinary, as to exult over a betrayed, a renowned and unconquered enemy, and to massacre him in cold blood, except that very Edward, who has subjected his countrymen to the endurance of those torments of internal remorse and shame, which proclaim the mean, dastardly, cruel, and ungenerous spirit of one of the kings of England, in all succeding ages.

"Three things," says John Blair, "unite to immortalize the fame of noble Wallace; his own innocence; the tyranny of Edward; and the treachery of Monteith."

Cruel tyranny usually defeats her own purposes. The ignoble and barbarous manner in which Wallace was treated, in instituting a mock trial by foreigners, fixing his divided body to the city gates of his native country, for which he bled and died, roused every spark of Caledonian valour and independence, exasperated the nation and animated them to revenge, and excited all the friends and admirers of Wallace to rally round the standard of Bruce, to avenge the death of Wallace, to shake off the yoke of such an inexorible tyrant, and to fill the Scottish throne with a lawful sovereign.

The innocence of the purest of mortals on earth could have no chance or protection in the presence of such an avaricious and sanguinary Monarch; and the treachery of a traitor, who betrays innocent blood and affects the happiness of a liberal nation can never be forgiven; it entails the greatest infamy on the name of his posterity, while the remembrance of his crime harbours in the minds of the nation.

POPULAR POETRY.

BYRON'S WORKS, COMPLETE, in Verse and Prose, containing his Letters. Royal octavo, 974 pages; bound in different styles, with engravings.

MILTON'S POETICAL WORKS, with a Memoir of the Author, and Critical Remarks, by James Montgomery; 36 engravings, from drawings by Wm. Harvey. 2 vols 12mo. on pica type, 806 pages.

MILTON'S PARADISE LOST, on pica type, and 10 fine illustrations—12mo.

POETICAL WORKS of Thomas Campbell; illustrated with 34 engravings, from designs by Harvey—octavo, on pica type, 358 pages.

POETS OF AMERICA, by George B. Cheever, D. D.—12mo., 406 pages; containing portraits of Bryant, Willis, Pierpont, Mrs. Sigourney, Halleck, Longfellow, and Allston—good paper, and well bound.

POEMS of John J. G. C. Brainard, from new stereotype plates; fine engravings; 221 pages. Copy-right book, and the only COMPLETE edition published.

COURSE OF TIME, by Robert Pollok, A. M.—With a Memoir of the Author, an Analysis of each Book, and a Comprehensive Index. The whole prepared expressly for this edition, by W. C. Armstrong—octavo, 322 pages, with engravings.

GEMS OF POETRY, from Forty-eight American Poets, with portraits of Halleck, Longfellow, Wm. C. Bryant, and N. P. Willis—252 pages, 12mo.

YOUNG'S NIGHT THOUGHTS, 18mo.—in various styles of binding.

HUDIBRAS, by Samuel Butler; with a Life of the Author—312 pages, 18mo:

ESSAY ON MAN, in Four Epistles, with the Universal Prayer, by Alexander Pope—18mo:

SONG BOOKS.

ÆOLIAN HARP, or Songsters' Cabinet; being a collection of Humorous, Sentimental and Popular Songs.

UNIVERSAL SONGSTER; containing a collection of National, Irish, Naval, Military, Sporting, Comic, Sentimental, and Amatory Songs—312 pages, 18mo.

New Song-Book, with 12 plates—126 pages, 18mo.

The Patriotic Song-Book, 468 pages, 18mo.

The Military " " 468 do. do.

The Naval " " 468 do. do

SCIENTIFIC AND HISTORICAL.

History, Diseases, and Treatment of the ***HORSE;*** embracing every variety of information relative to this noble animal illustrated with more than 100 engravings.—The above has just been reprinted in one large octavo volume, com prising nearly 500 pages, and containing much valuable matter in regard to Breeding, Breaking, Training, Shoeing, Bad Habits, and the general management of Horses Price $2 50.

COMBE on the Constitution of Man; Essays on Decision of Character, &c., by John Foster, Esq.; *Philosophy of Sleep* and *Anatomy of Drunkenness*, by Robert Macnish, Esq.; *Influence of Literature upon Society*, &c., by Madame de Stael; and *A Treatise on Self-Knowledge*, by John Mason, A. M.—5 works in one vol. royal octavo.

SURGEON AND PHYSICIAN, designed to assist heads of Families, Travellers and Seafaring people, in discerning and curing Diseases, by W. M. Hand: with an Introduction, by J. L. Comstock, M. D.—12mo:

WALKER ON BEAUTY, or Beauty Illustrated, chiefly by an Analysis and Classification of Beauty in Woman; by Alexander Walker, author of Intermarriage, Women, &c. &c.—edited by an American Physician.

WALKER ON WOMAN, or Woman Physiologically Considered, as to Mind, Morals, Marriage, Matrimonial Slavery, Infidelity, and Divorce; by Alexander Walker, With an Appendix, edited by an American Physician.

PALEY'S PHILOSOPHY, or the Principles of Moral and Political Philosophy, by Wm. Paley, D. D.—2 vols.

CHAPTALL'S CHEMISTRY—12mo., 365 pages.

TAYLOR AND HIS GENERALS; containing a Biography of Major General Zachary Taylor, and Sketches of the Lives of Generals Worth, Wool, and Twiggs; with a full Account of the various Actions of their Divisions in Mexico; together with a sketch of the life of Major General Scott—Embellished with 12 portraits and engravings on tinted paper—12mo., 326 pages.

MEXICO and Her Military Chieftains, from the revolution of Hidalgo to the present time; comprising Sketches of the Lives of Hidalgo, Morelos, Iturbide, Santa Anna, Paredes, Almonte, Arista, Ampudia, Herrera, and De la Vega; by Fay Robinson—Illustrated by 12 portraits and engravings on tinted paper—12mo., 344 pages.

BONAPARTE'S Campaign in Russia; containing a faithful description of the distressing and interesting scenes of which the author was an eye-witness; by Eugene Labaume; translated from the French—octavo, 348 pages.

www.ingramcontent.com/pod-product-compliance
Lightning Source LLC
LaVergne TN
LVHW021416110826
845150LV00007B/1951

* 9 7 8 1 4 2 5 5 1 0 0 1 5 *